Contents

Introduction

UNDERSTANDING CANNABIS is Volume 328 in the **ISSUES** series. The aim of the series is to offer current, diverse information about important issues in our world, from a UK perspective.

ABOUT UNDERSTANDING CANNABIS

Cannabis (also known as marijuana, weed, dope or grass) is the most used illegal drug in the UK. This book explores the effects the drug can have on a person and the possible brain damage which can be caused. It looks at the arguments both for and against legalisation of the drug in the UK. It also explores the medicinal uses of cannabis and the conditions it is sometimes used to treat.

OUR SOURCES

Titles in the **ISSUES** series are designed to function as educational resource books, providing a balanced overview of a specific subject.

The information in our books is comprised of facts, articles and opinions from many different sources, including:

⇨ Newspaper reports and opinion pieces

⇨ Website factsheets

⇨ Magazine and journal articles

⇨ Statistics and surveys

⇨ Government reports

⇨ Literature from special interest groups.

A NOTE ON CRITICAL EVALUATION

Because the information reprinted here is from a number of different sources, readers should bear in mind the origin of the text and whether the source is likely to have a particular bias when presenting information (or when conducting their research). It is hoped that, as you read about the many aspects of the issues explored in this book, you will critically evaluate the information presented.

It is important that you decide whether you are being presented with facts or opinions. Does the writer give a biased or unbiased report? If an opinion is being expressed, do you agree with the writer? Is there potential bias to the 'facts' or statistics behind an article?

ASSIGNMENTS

In the back of this book, you will find a selection of assignments designed to help you engage with the articles you have been reading and to explore your own opinions. Some tasks will take longer than others and there is a mixture of design, writing and research-based activities that you can complete alone or in a group.

Useful weblinks

www.adamsmith.org

www.bristol.ac.uk

www.christian.org.uk

www.drugabuse.gov

www.emcdda.europa.eu

www.epilepsy.org.uk

www.espad.org

www.huffingtonpost.co.uk

www.independent.co.uk

www.ibtimes.co.uk

www.kcl.ac.uk

www.nhs.uk

www.samafoundation.org

www.theconversation.com

www.theguardian.com

www.the telegraph.co.uk

www.tri.org

www.yougov.co.uk

FURTHER RESEARCH

At the end of each article we have listed its source and a website that you can visit if you would like to conduct your own research. Please remember to critically evaluate any sources that you consult and consider whether the information you are viewing is accurate and unbiased.

Understanding Cannabis

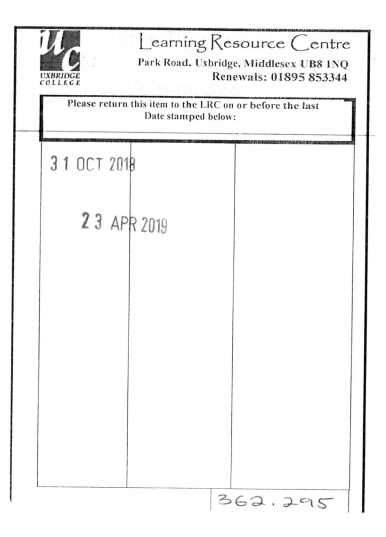

Independence Educational Publishers

First published by Independence Educational Publishers

The Studio, High Green

Great Shelford

Cambridge CB22 5EG

England

ISBN-13: 978 1 86168 779 1

Printed in Great Britain

Zenith Print Group

Cannabis: the facts

Cannabis (also known as marijuana, weed, dope or grass) is the most widely used illegal drug in the UK, although its use in recent years has fallen.

The proportion of 11–15 year olds in England who had used cannabis in the last year fell from 13.3% in 2003 to 7% in 2013. The proportion of 16–59 year olds using cannabis in the last year has fallen from 10.6% in 2003–04 to 6.6% in 2013–14.

How cannabis makes you feel

The effects of cannabis vary from person to person:

⇨ some people may feel chilled out, relaxed and happy

⇨ others get the giggles or become more talkative

⇨ hunger pangs are common – this is sometimes known as "getting the munchies"

⇨ you may become more aware of your senses – colours may look more intense and music may sound better

⇨ it's common to feel as though time is slowing down.

Cannabis can have other effects too:

⇨ it makes some people feel faint and/or sick – this is sometimes known as a "whitey"

⇨ it can make you feel sleepy and lethargic

⇨ some people find it affects their memory, making it harder to remember things

⇨ it makes some people feel confused, anxious or paranoid, and some experience panic attacks and hallucinations. These effects are particularly common with stronger forms of cannabis, such as skunk and sinsemilla

If you use cannabis regularly it can make you demotivated and uninterested in other things going on in your life, such as education or work. Long-term use can affect your ability to learn and to concentrate.

Can you get addicted to cannabis?

In the past cannabis wasn't thought to be addictive. However, research has shown that it can be addictive, particularly if you have been using it regularly for quite a while. About 10% of regular cannabis users are thought to become dependent.

As with other addictive drugs such as cocaine and heroin, you can develop a tolerance to it. This means you have to have more and more to get the same effects. If you stop taking it, you can experience withdrawal symptoms, such as cravings, difficulty sleeping, mood swings, irritability and restlessness.

"If you regularly smoke cannabis with tobacco, you're likely to get addicted to nicotine and may develop tobacco-related illnesses, such as cancer and coronary heart disease. If you cut down or give up, you will experience withdrawal from nicotine as well as cannabis"

Risks associated with cannabis

Recent research has helped us better understand the health risks from using cannabis. We know that:

⇨ **Cannabis affects your ability to drive**. This is one of the reasons why drug driving, like drink driving, is illegal. One French study found that drivers who had been using cannabis were more than twice as likely to cause a fatal car crash.

⇨ **If you smoke it, cannabis can be harmful to your lungs**. Like tobacco, it contains cancer-causing chemicals (carcinogens) that increase your risk of lung cancer. It can also make asthma worse, and cause wheezing in people without asthma. If you mix cannabis with tobacco and smoke it, the risks to your lungs are higher.

⇨ **Cannabis can harm your mental health**. Regular use is associated with an increased risk of developing a psychotic illness, such as schizophrenia. A psychotic illness is one where you experience hallucinations (when you see things that aren't really there) and delusions (when you believe things that aren't really true). Your risk of developing a psychotic illness is higher if you start using cannabis in your teens and if you have a family history of mental illness. Cannabis use has also been shown to increase the risk of a relapse in people who have schizophrenia, and could make existing symptoms worse.

⇨ **Cannabis may affect your fertility**. Research done in animals suggests that cannabis can disrupt sperm production in males and ovulation in females.

⇨ **If you are pregnant, cannabis may harm your unborn baby**. Research suggests that using cannabis during pregnancy could affect your baby's brain development. Regularly smoking cannabis with tobacco is associated with an increased risk of your baby being born small or premature.

Does my age affect my risks?

The risks linked to using cannabis do seem to be higher for people who use it regularly from an early age, including the risk of developing a mental illness.

It's not clear why the risks are higher for people who start using cannabis when young. It may be linked to the fact that, during the teenage years, the brain is still forming its connections and cannabis interferes with this process.

Does cannabis have medicinal benefits?

Herbal cannabis contains many different compounds, called cannabinoids, which have different effects. Two of these cannabinoids – tetrahydrocannabinol (THC) and cannabidiol (CBD) – are the active ingredients of a prescribed drug called Sativex. Currently this is only licensed in the UK as a treatment to relieve the pain of muscle spasms in multiple sclerosis.

Further research is under way to test the effectiveness of cannabis-based drugs for a range of other conditions including the eye disease glaucoma, appetite loss in people with HIV or AIDS, epilepsy in children and pain associated with cancer. We won't know whether or not these treatments are effective until trials have concluded

Does cannabis lead to other drugs?

While most people who use harder drugs like heroin have used cannabis, only a small proportion of people who use cannabis go on to use hard drugs. However, buying cannabis brings you into contact with the illegal drugs trade, making it more likely that you will be exposed to other drugs.

Where can I get more information about cannabis?

You'll find more information about cannabis in the Frank website's A–Z of drugs.

If you need support with giving up cannabis, you'll find sources of help in *Drugs: where to get help*.

Content reviewed August 2017

⇨ The above information is reprinted with kind permission from NHS Choices. Please visit www.nhs.uk for further information.

Study shows white matter damage may be caused by 'skunk-like' cannabis

Smoking high potency 'skunk-like' cannabis can damage a crucial part of the brain responsible for communication between the two brain hemispheres, according to a new study by scientists from King's College London and Sapienza University of Rome.

Researchers have known for some time that long-term cannabis use increases the risk of psychosis, and recent evidence suggests that alterations in brain function and structure may be responsible for this greater vulnerability. However, this new research, published today in *Psychological Medicine*, is the first to examine the effect of cannabis potency on brain structure.

Exploring the impact of cannabis potency is particularly important since today's high potency 'skunk-like products have been shown to contain higher proportions of Δ9-tetrahydrocannabinol (THC) than they did around a decade ago. In experimental studies THC has been shown to induce psychotic symptoms and 'skunk-like' products high in THC are now thought to be the most commonly used form of cannabis in the UK.

Dr Paola Dazzan, Reader in Neurobiology of Psychosis from the Institute of Psychiatry, Psychology & Neuroscience (IoPPN) at King's College London, and senior researcher on the study, said: "'We found that frequent use of high potency cannabis significantly affects the structure of white matter fibres in the brain, whether you have psychosis or not.

"This reflects a sliding scale where the more cannabis you smoke and the higher the potency, the worse the damage will be."

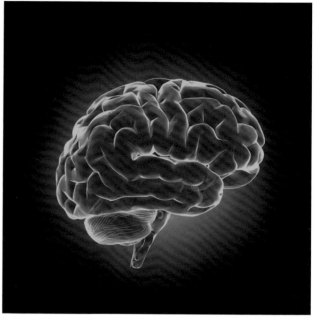

Diffusion Tensor Imaging (DTI), a Magnetic Resonance Imaging (MRI) technique, was used to examine white matter in the brains of 56 patients who had reported a first episode of psychosis at the South London and Maudsley NHS Foundation Trust (SLaM), as well as 43 healthy participants from the local community.

The researchers specifically examined the corpus callosum, the largest white matter structure in the brain, which is responsible for communication between the left and right hemispheres. White matter consists of large bundles of nerve cell projections (called axons), which connect different regions of the brain, enabling communication between them.

The corpus callosum is particularly rich in cannabinoid receptors, on which the THC content of cannabis acts.

The study found that frequent use of high potency cannabis was linked to significantly higher mean-diffusivity (MD), a marker of damage in white matter structure.

Dr Tiago Reis Marques, a senior research fellow from the IoPPN at King's College London, said: "This white matter damage was significantly greater among heavy users of high potency cannabis than in occasional or low potency users, and was also independent of the presence of a psychotic disorder.'

Dr Dazzan added: "There is an urgent need to educate health professionals, the public and policymakers about the risks involved with cannabis use.

"As we have suggested previously, when assessing cannabis use it is extremely important to gather information on how often and what type of cannabis is being used. These details can help quantify the risk of mental health problems and increase awareness on the type of damage these substances can do to the brain."

This research was funded primarily by the NIHR Biomedical Research Centre at the South London and Maudsley (SLaM) NHS Foundation Trust and King's College London.

The study was led by Dr Tiago Reis Marques and Dr Paola Dazzan of the IoPPN at King's, and Dr Silvia Rigucci of Sapienza University of Rome.

27 November 2015

⇨ The above information is reprinted with kind permission from King's College, London. Please visit www.kcl.ac.uk for further information.

Four times as many men as women are diagnosed with cannabis psychosis

An article from The Conversation.

Ian Hamilton, Lecturer in Mental Health at University of York and Paul Galdas, Senior Lecturer in Adult Nursing at University of York

The journey from first using cannabis through to developing mental health problems is very different for men and women. Men outnumber women at every point along the way. Despite these marked gender differences, little attention has been paid to such a basic demographic factor in cannabis psychosis and the underlying reasons for why men fare so poorly.

The first clue might be found in who uses cannabis. The most comprehensive survey of drug use in the UK shows a consistent trend of twice as many men than women reporting that they have used cannabis. But no one really knows why there is a marked variation between the genders when it comes to using cannabis. Some have suggested that drug use carries more social stigma for women than men, and that younger men are also more likely than women to engage in risk-taking behaviour including illicit drug use. Others have said that men are more likely to use drugs and alcohol as a coping mechanism, while women tend to cope with stress by using social support. Differences in the rates of psychosis unrelated to cannabis also mirror the gender differences evident in cannabis users, with males outnumbering females by a ratio of two to one.

Cannabis has been linked to psychosis for some time and although the debate continues as to the exact nature of the relationship, many people require health and social care for the problems they experience. However, it is interesting that despite the widespread attention that researchers have paid to cannabis psychosis there has yet to be a large-scale analysis of the role gender in the condition. To date, seminal research on this issue has focused disproportionately on men or on small samples.

We analysed admissions to hospital in England and found that men are four times more likely than women to be diagnosed with cannabis psychosis. These elevated rates were consistent over the 11 years of the study period.

Bias in treatment

So what might account for this widening of the gender ratio? There are a number of plausible explanations. It could be the result of a bias in treatment services which tend to be dominated by male patients. This is in some ways also linked to the long-standing bias in research involving samples of men because research samples are often drawn from treatment settings out of convenience.

"It is also likely that women with children will avoid seeking specialist treatment when they develop mental health problems as a result of cannabis use due to the fear that their children may be taken into care, particularly if they have no family support"

Staff working in mental health services may have also become more attentive to problems associated with cannabis use, and the greater number of men diagnosed and treated for cannabis psychosis may therefore reflect the disproportionate number of men who currently receive treatment for mental health problems. Paradoxically, the excessive number of male patients in services can act as a barrier to women who need treatment, as they frequently have a history of trauma and exploitation perpetrated by men.

Likewise, services may be treating such women differently knowing that they have a duty to safeguard these children. Consequently, health and social care services might be offering alternatives to hospital treatment such as community services as a way of maintaining continued contact between mother and child.

"And then there is biology, which may also have a role to play. Research has suggested that the female hormone oestrogen may have a protective effect for women in relation to psychosis"

Despite all the unknowns when it comes to cannabis psychosis, gender clearly matters. As well as treating men and reducing the number of people with psychosis, what we now need to work out is whether there are women we need to reach and how best to do it.

27 August 2015

⇨ The above information is reprinted with kind permission from *The Conversation*. Please visit www.theconversation.com for further information.

Clever teenagers twice as likely to smoke cannabis due to their curious minds, study finds

Camilla Turner, Education Editor

Students who are high academic achievers at age 11 are also more likely to drink alcohol as teenagers, according to a nine-year study by University College London (UCL).

Experts examined data for more than 6,059 young people from 838 state and 52 public schools across England. They found that bright children are less likely to smoke cigarettes as teenagers but more likely to smoke cannabis.

This could be because middle class parents pay more attention to health warnings about cigarettes, which they pass on to their children.

Researchers found that clever children are more likely to smoke cannabis in their late teenage years because they have greater curiosity and strive to be accepted by older people.

They added that children who are "initially cautious of illegal substances in early adolescence as they are more aware of the immediate and long-term repercussions that breaking the law may incur than those with lower academic ability."

Scientists gathered information on the academic achievement of children at age 11 and compared it with their behaviour during early adolescence, defined as age 13–17, and then late adolescence, defined as age 18–20.

During their late teenage years, clever children were more than twice as likely to drink alcohol regularly and persistently than those who were not as clever.

Meanwhile, clever pupils were 50% more likely to use cannabis occasionally and nearly twice as likely to use it persistently than their less gifted peers.

Researchers found that these patterns persisted into adulthood and appear to contradict the notion that academic prowess was associated with a greater tendency to 'experiment' temporarily with these substances.

"High childhood academic at age 11 is associated with a reduced risk of cigarette smoking but an increased risk of drinking alcohol regularly and cannabis use," the researchers, from University College London, wrote.

"These associations persist into early adulthood, providing evidence against the hypothesis that high academic ability is associated with temporary 'experimentation' with substance use."

The study, published in the journal *BMJ Open*, found that during their early teens, high-achieving pupils were less likely to smoke cigarettes than their less gifted peers. And they were more likely to say they drank alcohol during this period.

Dr James Williams at UCL Medical School said there has been a general downward trend in smoking cannabis and drinking alcohol among teenagers.

He added: "These risky health behaviours present a large problem in terms of public health as substance use is a risk factor for immediate and long-term health problems, as well as negative non-health outcomes such as poor educational and employment outcomes.

"The outcomes of cannabis use were found to be worsened by early onset and increased frequency of use.

"Understanding the risk factors for adolescent substance use can inform public health policymaking and help target interventions for those in high-risk groups."

23 February 2017

⇨ The above information is reprinted with kind permission from *The Telegraph*. Please visit www.the telegraph.co.uk for further information.

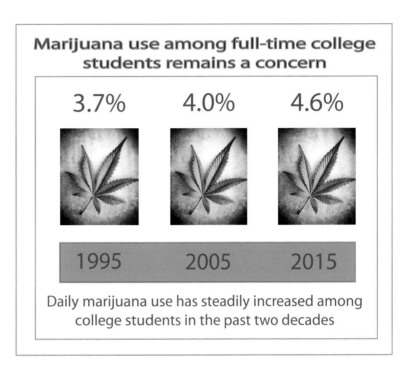

Marijuana use among full-time college students remains a concern

3.7%   4.0%   4.6%

1995   2005   2015

Daily marijuana use has steadily increased among college students in the past two decades

Edible marijuana: what we need to know

***An article from* The Conversation.**

By Margie Skeer, Assistant Professor of Public Health and Community Medicine, Tufts University

Marijuana-infused foods – often called edibles – are becoming more and more popular in states such as Colorado, where recreational marijuana is sold.

In the first quarter of 2014, the first year recreational sales were allowed in Colorado, edibles made up 30 per cent of legal sales. By the third quarter of 2016, that grew to 45 per cent.

Edibles come in a variety of forms, from candy and baked goods, to trail mix and even coffee or soda.

As a social and behavioural scientist who studies the prevention of adolescent substance initiation and misuse, the legalisation of recreational marijuana has been on my mind a lot lately. The younger people are when they start using substances, the greater the risk for developing subsequent neurocognitive, mental health and further substance-related problems.

Marijuana-infused edibles raise a lot of concerns. Young children may accidentally eat edibles meant to look like candy or other foods, and adolescents may not think edibles are as risky as smoking marijuana.

Concerns about edibles

Edibles are manufactured with varying levels of tetrahydrocannabinol (THC), the active ingredient in marijuana. They can take the form of almost any type of food, most notably candy and baked goods.

When products are shaped like candy, there is a concern that children will accidentally ingest them. They may mistake these marijuana-infused products for regular food, as they may not be able to read the labels and markings indicating that the products contain THC, or may not understand what the labels actually mean.

A recent retrospective study examined unintentional exposure to marijuana among children who were treated at a children's hospital and regional poison centre in Colorado between 2009 and 2015, the year after it became legal for recreational marijuana to be sold in the state.

Findings indicated a five-fold increase in the number of children under ten who were exposed to marijuana, from nine cases in 2009 to 47 cases in 2015. The poison centre saw an average increase of 34 per cent, while there was an average increase of 19 per cent for the rest of the country.

Edibles were implicated in over half of the exposures, which included baked goods, candy and popcorn products.

Teens may accidentally ingest edibles as well. In these cases, though, the concern is that teens may give edibles to their peers without telling them what is in the product.

Risk perception of edibles is lower

In 2015, only 12.3 per cent of high school seniors believed that trying marijuana once or twice was harmful (down from 18.5 per cent in 2009). Less than one in three believed smoking marijuana regularly to be harmful, down from 52.4 per cent in 2009.

My professional opinion is that marijuana-infused edibles will continue to push down this trend in perceived risk among adolescents, as edibles may appear much less risky than smokable forms. In other words, it is a much shorter leap from not using marijuana at all to eating an edible product to get high, compared to the leap between no use and smoking the drug for the first time through a joint or a bong.

Additionally, edibles make it significantly easier for those who are underage to use marijuana covertly,

EDIBLE

which may make it more appealing. This could potentially increase frequency of use.

The risk of getting caught using marijuana at home or at school may be lower if an adolescent is eating a cookie or candy infused with THC than smoking the drug. That could make this mode of use appealing for teens who may otherwise abstain out of the fear of repercussions associated with "smelling like pot".

Recent qualitative research found that some teens did use edibles in school specifically for this reason. Moreover, some of the females reported that they found edibles appealing because using the drug in this manner made them less likely to appear in public as a "marijuana user".

How much THC is in that cookie?

Dosing is another concern. Colorado and Washington state have set a limit of ten milligrams per individual serving, while Oregon and Alaska set a limit of five milligrams for an individual serving. In theory, regulations surrounding dosing in specific milligram increments would be helpful in allowing consumers to self-regulate how much they ingest.

The size of the dose is one issue, but how it is administered is another. If a drug is inhaled, it is quickly absorbed into the bloodstream and then goes to the brain. This is the fastest way of administering a drug.

The slowest mode of administration is ingestion, such as through pills or food. The drug enters the bloodstream through the lining of the stomach and small intestine, and then has to travel to the brain. This means it can take about 30–60 minutes to feel the effects. Eating a product with a drug in it may take even longer, because the body has to digest it as food first before the substance gets into the lining of the stomach.

A person who is not aware of this delay might eat more after not initially feeling the effects, thinking that the drug will take effect faster, not recognising the potential harms associated with the increased dosage.

There are also different types of marijuana, specifically sativa and indica. Sativa has a more stimulating, energetic effect, whereas indica has more of a psychoactive and sedating effect. There are also hybrids of the two, if users are interested in a combination of the different effects.

However, research on marijuana has been limited, so not much has been examined with the different types and different strains, especially among adolescents, making it a challenge to understand the full picture.

Policies regarding edibles

Like all marijuana, cannabis-infused edibles are not regulated by the FDA. At the moment, polices and regulations about edibles are being drafted by states that are voting to legalise recreational marijuana.

The states with the longest history of legalised recreational marijuana, Colorado and Washington, have the most extensive policies surrounding edibles. As problems associated with the recreational use of marijuana have surfaced, these policies have – and continue to – change.

For example, in response to the increased number of children being admitted to hospitals as a result of ingesting edible marijuana, Colorado enacted a policy in October 2016 requiring that a universal symbol be put on all edible marijuana products to make it clear that they contain THC. In addition, the word candy is not allowed on edible marijuana packaging, and manufacturing edibles in shapes that are appealing to children (such as gummy bears) is also banned.

Washington has strict and extensive policies around edibles, including explicit language that needs to be put on labels and packaging. The state also bans images on packaging that would appeal to young children, such as cartoons and toys, as well as edible candy that would be most appealing to young people, such as gummy bears and jelly beans.

California, Maine, Massachusetts and Nevada all voted to legalise recreational marijuana in the 2016 election.

California's Prop. 64, the ballot proposition for recreational marijuana restricts edibles with a ten milligram portion size requirement, and additional requirements that packaging be childproof and, as with other states, not to appeal to children.

Maine, Massachusetts and Nevada are drafting legislation to regulate recreational sales of marijuana, including edibles.

Where do we go from here?

As a professional in this field, I understand the desire to offer multiple routes of administration of marijuana, particularly for those who are using it for medical reasons.

However, I believe that edible marijuana, especially in forms that are appealing to young people, is extremely problematic.

Adolescent substance misuse prevention professionals have their work cut out for them, as prevention efforts will have to specifically target marijuana edibles moving forward. Additionally, it is up to policymakers to do everything in their power to make it harder for those who are under 21 to acquire and also consume edible marijuana. This will require a lot of time preparing before the policies go into effect.

1 March 2017

⇨ The above information is reprinted with kind permission from *The Conversation*. Please visit www.theconversation.com for further information.

Long-term pot use can alter your brain's circuitry, study finds

Chronic use can alter your reward centers.

By Yagana Shah

After years of recreational marijuana use, you might experience changes in the pathway of your brain – also known as the reward system of your brain, a new study says.

Simply put, researchers from the University of Texas at Dallas, Center for Brain Health found that – over time – the drug can disrupt your brain.

A small study of 59 adult long-term marijuana users and 70 non-users had participants self-report their urges to use the drug after being shown various photos. The photos included things like pot paraphernalia, including bongs, joints and pipes, along with what researchers considered "natural rewards", such as pieces of fruit, including apples, oranges and bananas.

The marijuana users had on average been consistently using the drug for around 12 years.

In the non-user group, researchers saw greater activity in the brain's reward centres using magnetic resonance imaging when they were shown pieces of fruit. In the marijuana user group, however, they found more activity across their brains' reward centres when shown pot-related photos compared with those of fruit.

"This study shows that marijuana disrupts the natural reward circuitry of the brain, making marijuana highly salient to those who use it heavily. In essence, these brain alterations could be a marker of transition from recreational marijuana use to problematic use," one of the study's authors, Francesca Filbey, said in a statement.

Recent data shows that marijuana use had increased in post 50s in the last decade.

While it's sometimes used medically for patients wishing to reduce symptoms of nausea and pain, other research has indicated the detrimental effects of long-term use. Use of the drug over a long period has been shown – in some studies – to reduce verbal memory and even the brain's processing speed.

Researchers say the new study findings could explain why some chronic marijuana users experience problems in their personal lives.

"We found that this disruption of the reward system correlates with the number of problems, such as family issues, individuals have because of their marijuana use," Filbey said. "Continued marijuana use despite these problems is an indicator of marijuana dependence."

8 June 2016

⇨ The above information is reprinted with kind permission from *The Huffington Post*. Please visit www.huffingtonpost.co.uk for further information.

Does marijuana affect your sleep?

An article from The Conversation.

THE CONVERSATION

Deirdre Conroy, Clinical Associate Professor of Psychiatry, University of Michigan.

If you speak to someone who has suffered from insomnia at all as an adult, chances are good that person has either tried using marijuana, or cannabis, for sleep or has thought about it.

This is reflected in the many variations of cannabinoid or cannabis-based medicines available to improve sleep – like Nabilone, Dronabinol and Marinol. It's also a common reason why many cannabis users seek medical marijuana cards.

I am a sleep psychologist who has treated hundreds of patients with insomnia, and it seems to me the success of cannabis as a sleep aid is highly individual. What makes cannabis effective for one person's sleep and not another's?

While there are still many questions to be answered, existing research suggests that the effects of cannabis on sleep may depend on many factors, including individual differences, cannabis concentrations and frequency of use.

Cannabis and sleep

Access to cannabis is increasing. As of last November, 28 U.S. states and the District of Columbia had legalized cannabis for medicinal purposes.

Research on the effects of cannabis on sleep in humans has largely been compiled of somewhat inconsistent studies conducted in the 1970s. Researchers seeking to learn how cannabis affects the sleeping brain have studied volunteers in the sleep laboratory and measured sleep stages and sleep continuity. Some studies showed that users' ability to fall and stay asleep improved. A small number of subjects also had a slight increase in slow wave sleep, the deepest stage of sleep.

However, once nightly cannabis use stops, sleep clearly worsens across the withdrawal period.

Over the past decade, research has focused more on the use of cannabis for

medical purposes. Individuals with insomnia tend to use medical cannabis for sleep at a high rate. Up to 65 percent of former cannabis users identified poor sleep as a reason for relapsing. Use for sleep is particularly common in individuals with PTSD and pain.

This research suggests that, while motivation to use cannabis for sleep is high, and might initially be beneficial to sleep, these improvements might wane with chronic use over time.

Does frequency matter?

We were interested in how sleep quality differs between daily cannabis users, occasional users who smoked at least once in the last month and people who don't smoke at all.

We asked 98 mostly young and healthy male volunteers to answer surveys, keep daily sleep diaries and wear accelerometers for one week. Accelerometers, or actigraphs, measure activity patterns across multiple days. Throughout the study, subjects used cannabis as they typically would.

Our results show that the frequency of use seems to be an important factor as it relates to the effects on sleep. Thirty-nine percent of daily users complained of clinically significant insomnia. Meanwhile, only 10 percent of occasional users had insomnia complaints. There were no differences in sleep complaints between nonusers and nondaily users.

Interestingly, when controlling for the presence of anxiety and depression, the differences disappeared. This suggests that cannabis's effect on sleep may differ depending on whether you have depression or anxiety. In order words, if you have depression, cannabis may help you sleep – but if you don't, cannabis may hurt.

Future directions

Cannabis is still a schedule I substance, meaning that the government does not consider cannabis to be medically therapeutic due to lack of research to support its benefits. This creates a barrier to research, as only one university in the country, University of Mississippi, is permitted by the National Institute of Drug Abuse to grow marijuana for research.

New areas for exploration in the field of cannabis research might examine how various cannabis subspecies influence sleep and how this may differ between individuals.

One research group has been exploring cannabis types or cannabinoid concentrations that are preferable depending on one's sleep disturbance. For example, one strain might relieve insomnia, while another can affect nightmares.

Other studies suggest that medical cannabis users with insomnia tend to prefer higher concentrations of cannabidiol, a nonintoxicating ingredient in cannabis.

This raises an important question. Should the medical community communicate these findings to patients with insomnia who inquire about medical cannabis? Some health professionals may not feel comfortable due to the fluctuating legal status, a lack of confidence in the state of the science or their personal opinions.

At this point, cannabis's effect on sleep seems highly variable, depending on the person, the timing of use, the cannabis type and concentration, mode of ingestion and other factors. Perhaps the future will yield more fruitful discoveries.

11 September 2017

⇨ The above information is reprinted with kind permission from *The Conversation*. Please visit www.theconversation.com for further information.

Boys who smoke cannabis "are four inches shorter"

Sarah Knapton, Science editor

New study finds that youngsters who regularly smoked marijuana are far shorter than their non-smoking peers

Boys who smoke cannabis before puberty could be stunting their growth by more than four inches, a new study suggests.

Researchers found that youngsters who were addicted to the drug were far shorter than their non-smoking peers.

And they also discovered that rather than being a relaxing pastime, smoking dope actually makes the body more stressed in the long term.

"Marijuana use may provoke a stress response that stimulates onset of puberty but suppresses growth rate," said study leader Dr Syed Shakeel Raza Rizvi, of the Agriculture University Rawalpindi in Pakistan.

Scientists at the Pir Mehr Ali Shah Agriculture University Rawalpindi in Pakistan studied the levels of certain hormones involved in growth and puberty in the blood of 220 non-smoking and 217 cannabis-addicted boys.

Levels of puberty-related hormones such as testosterone and luteinising hormone (LH) were increased in the cannabis smokers. In contrast, growth hormone levels in the group were decreased.

⇨ Super strong cannabis responsible for quarter of psychosis cases

⇨ Cannabis use shrinks and rewires the brain

⇨ Even casual use of cannabis alters the brain

⇨ Cannabis can be highly addictive, major study finds

It was also found that non-smoking boys were on average four kilos heavier and 4.6 inches taller by the age of 20 than the dope smokers.

The researchers also looked at the effect of smoking cannabis on levels of the stress hormone, cortisol, in ten cannabis addicts.

They found that dope smokers have significantly higher levels of cortisol than non-smokers.

Cannabis is the most widely available illicit drug in Europe, and it's estimated that it's been used by 80.5 million Europeans at least once in their life.

The proportion of 11–15-year-olds in England who had used cannabis in the last year fell from 13.3 per cent in 2003 to seven per cent in 2013, around 250,000 youngsters.

The latest report from the European Monitoring Centre for Drugs and Drug Addiction (EMCDDA) reveals that the highest prevalence of cannabis use is among 15- to 24-year-olds and is significantly higher among men than women.

Previous studies have looked at the effect of smoking cannabis in adult rats and humans, but this is the first time that the effects have been looked at in prepubescent boys.

Dr Rivzi said the the research may have a wider impact than just health, adding: "Early puberty is associated with younger age of onset of drinking and smoking, and early maturers have higher levels of substance abuse because they enter the risk period at an early level of emotional maturity."

The researchers say their findings, presented at the European Congress of Endocrinology in Dublin, will lead to a better understanding of the dangers of drug abuse on growth and development in children.

19 May 2015

⇨ The above information is reprinted with kind permission from *The Telegraph*. Please visit www. thetelegraph.co.uk for further information.

Remind me again, how does cannabis affect the brain?

THE CONVERSATION

An article from **The Conversation.**

Murat Yücel, Professor and Clinical Neuropyschogist, Monash University; Aaron Kandola, Research Assistant, Monash Clinical and Imaging Neuroscience, Monash University; and Adrian Carter, Senior Research Fellow, Monash University

Governments and communities worldwide are softening their views on cannabis use. Trials of medicinal cannabis have been approved in Victoria, Queensland and New South Wales. And the Australian parliament is currently debating legislation to introduce a government regulator of medicinal cannabis.

This follows decriminalisation of cannabis in Portugal and its legalisation in Uruguay and several US states.

Cannabis is still the product of choice for many illicit drug users in Australia. Five times as many people use cannabis rather than cocaine or methamphetamines.

But debate remains about the long-term effect the drug has on the brain, cognition and mental health. Most cannabis users start as teenagers and there is a widespread perception that this can disrupt critical developmental processes to leave a lasting negative impact on the brain.

Let's look at what the latest research has to say about the long-term harms, whether they can be reversed, and the possibility of making the drug safer.

How does it affect the developing brain?

Studies have shown that individuals who begin regular and heavy cannabis use in their teenage years have a lower level of educational attainment and IQ, earn a lower wage, and are more likely to engage in heavy alcohol or hard drug use, suffer from metal health problems, or end up in prison.

Heavy cannabis use – defined as daily use for at least one year – is consistently associated with poorer attention and memory, as well as earlier and increased rates of metal health problems, especially psychotic symptoms.

Researchers have also identified differences in the brain associated with these cognitive and mental health impairments.

However, there are a range of factors that can influence cognition, mental health and brain structure. These include age, use of other substances, rate of exercise, education level, family history, childhood abuse and neglect, pre-existing neurological differences, and the chemical composition of the cannabis itself.

It's often not possible to account for all these factors when undertaking cannabis research. So it's difficult to tell how much of the difference in a participants' performance on a cognitive task, mental health and brain structure is attributable to their level of cannabis use and how much can be explained by other factors.

Are the impairments reversible?

We are only just beginning to understand how well-equipped the human brain is for adapting to environmental demands or stresses. This capacity, known as brain plasticity, means that our brain is constantly striving to optimise its functioning, even when it is damaged or injured.

A stroke, for instance, can harm certain areas of the brain but it is possible that at least some functioning of that region may be restored as neural connections are rewired in an attempt to compensate for the damage.

Similar recovery mechanisms may operate in cases where the brain has been harmed from long-term and heavy cannabis exposure. Though just a handful of researchers have investigated this possibility in the context of cognition.

One large-scale study conducted over eight years found that heavy cannabis use was associated with memory impairments, but individuals had shown improvements in their memory once they stopped using the drug.

Other studies have shown that as little as three to six weeks of abstinence was sufficient for memory improvements.

Yet another study found no cognitive deficits in former users after only three months of abstinence.

Heavy cannabis use has also been suggested to disrupt neural functioning associated with memory. But again, a six-week period of abstinence was sufficient to show some recovery at the neural level.

However, a large study that followed cannabis users over nearly four decades found that there are limits to the ability of the brain to recover in those who begin using during early adolescence. Although cognition was improved in long-term cannabis users after 12 months of abstinence, cognitive impairments did persist, particularly in those who began using cannabis early.

Surprisingly, no studies to date have investigated whether the persistent effects of heavy cannabis use on brain structure can also recover with abstinence.

Stimulating brain plasticity is a major interest to neuroscientists. Some of the interventions to induce plasticity may facilitate the recovery from heavy cannabis use. Exercise is well established in promoting brain health, including the growth and development of neurons. It is possible that reversing cannabis-related harm through abstinence could be augmented with interventions such as exercise.

But while there is some evidence for recovery of function, it's an area that remains inconsistent and under-studied. More research is required before such an idea could bear any practical significance.

What's in your cannabis?

Cannabis contains a wide variety of psychoactive substances. The most prominent are the cannabinoids D9-tetrahydrocannabinol (THC) and cannabidiol (CBD).

Police seizures indicate there has been a sharp rise in the level of THC relative to CBD in smoked cannabis in recent decades. This could be due to a number of factors such as changes in the way people are growing the plant, using the different parts of the plant, or how they are preparing it for use.

THC is responsible for the 'high' associated with cannabis, but also causes psychotic symptoms and cognitive impairments. CBD is believed to limit the adverse impact of THC on the brain. But we don't know what proportion of CBD is necessary to mitigate these adverse effects. Nor do we know the extent to which these effects can be mitigated by CBD alone.

The creation of a well-regulated cannabis market, as has occurred in Colorado, may give researchers access

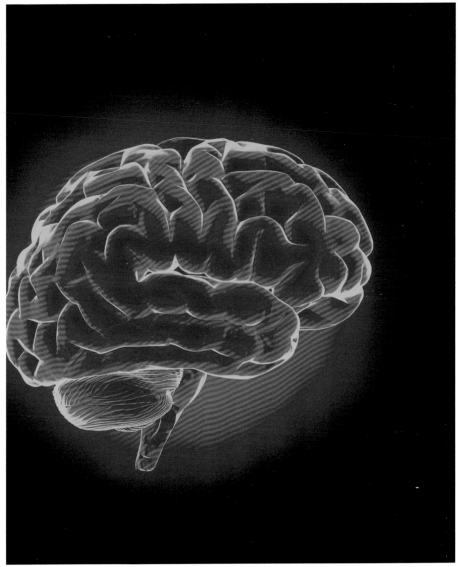

to reliable information about the chemical composition of the cannabis that an individual is consuming. This will make it possible to directly investigate whether CBD has a role to play in limiting the damage or even aiding recovery from the cannabis-related harm to the brain from heavy use.

Establishing the long-term impact of cannabis on the brain is a research priority for neuroscientists. Answers are needed to largely untouched questions such as whether any potential harm could be reversed (through exercise or other interventions) and whether increasing the concentration of CBD can limit the negative impact caused by cannabis high in THC.

The legislative changes poised to increase the availability of cannabis are

outpacing our understanding of the impact that the drug has on the brain. Without addressing these shortfalls in our knowledge, a fully informed debate about the likely consequences of increased cannabis use, whether it be for medical or recreational use, will not be possible.

27 May 2015

⇨ The above information is reprinted with kind permission from *The Conversation*. Please visit www.theconversation.com for further information.

ESPAD Report 2015

An extract from the European School Survey Project on Alcohol and Other Drugs.

The main purpose of the European School Survey Project on Alcohol and Other Drugs (ESPAD) is to collect comparable data on substance use among 15- to 16-year-old students in order to monitor trends within as well as between countries.

Any drug use

Lifetime use of illicit drugs varied considerably across the ESPAD countries. In the Czech Republic, 37% of the students reported having used any illicit drug at least once, which was more than twice the ESPAD average of 18%. Students in Bulgaria, France, Liechtenstein and Monaco also exhibit high levels of drug use experience (30–32%). Particularly low levels (10% or less) of illicit drug use were noted in Albania, Cyprus, the Faroes, Finland, the former Yugoslav Republic of Macedonia, Iceland, Moldova, Montenegro, Norway, Sweden and Ukraine. On average, 21% of boys and 15% of girls have tried illicit drugs at least once during their lifetime. In most ESPAD countries, prevalence rates were higher among boys than among girls. Noticeable gender differences were found in Georgia (24% for boys and 6% for girls), Liechtenstein (40% versus 23%) and Albania (18% versus 4%).

Cannabis use

The most prevalent illicit drug in all ESPAD countries is cannabis. On average, 16% of the students have used cannabis at least once in their lifetime. The country with the highest prevalence of cannabis use was the Czech Republic (37%). High prevalence rates (30 % or more) were also reported in France, Liechtenstein and Monaco. The lowest levels of cannabis use (4–7%) were reported in Albania, Cyprus, the Faroes, the former Yugoslav Republic of Macedonia, Iceland, Moldova, Norway and Sweden. On average, boys reported cannabis use to a larger extent than girls (19% versus 14%). This was the case in nearly all countries except the Czech Republic, the Faroes, Hungary, Iceland, Malta, Slovenia and Sweden, where rates were about the same for boys and girls. The largest gender differences (ten percentage points or more, higher rates among boys) were found in Albania, Georgia and Liechtenstein.

Other illicit drug use

Besides cannabis, some students have also used other illicit substances. In some cases, they have done so without any experience of cannabis at all. Among the most frequently tried illicit drugs are ecstasy, amphetamine, cocaine and LSD or other hallucinogens. In the case of illicit drugs other than cannabis, on average, 1–2% of the ESPAD students reported having used them at least once.

Lifetime prevalence rates for methamphetamine, crack, heroin and GHB were lower than those for the other illicit drugs (1% on average). At the country level, higher rates (5% or more) were found in Bulgaria (ecstasy, amphetamine, methamphetamine, cocaine) and Poland (LSD or other hallucinogens). The most marked gender differences are seen in Georgia (ecstasy: 7% for boys and 1% for girls) and Albania (cocaine: 6% versus 1%).

⇨ The above extract is reprinted with kind permission from The European School Survey Project on Alcohol and Other Drugs. Please visit www.espad.org for further information.

© The European School Survey Project on Alcohol and Other Drugs 2018

ESPAD average Perceived availability of substances (%)a			
	Average	Min.	Max.
Cigarettes	61	22	80
Alcohol	78	52	96
Cannabis	30	5	50
Ecstasy	12	2	24
Amphetamine	9	2	23
Methamphetamine	7	1	17
Cocaine	11	2	19
Crack	8	1	14

a Percentage of students rating a substance as either 'fairly easly' or 'very easy' to obtain.

Young people twice as relaxed about cannabis safety as adults

Young people think cannabis is as safe as adults think alcohol is – but cannabis is seen as twice as safe in America.

Will Dahlgreen

Young people think cannabis is as safe as adults think alcohol is – but cannabis is seen as twice as safe in America

11% of young people say magic mushrooms are safe; greater than the 8% of adults who say tobacco is safe. And men seem more relaxed about drug safety, with 41% saying alcohol is safe compared to 29% of women, and 25% saying cannabis is safe compared to 17% of women.

Despite ramped up advertising on the ill effects of smoking, young people (18%) are still twice as likely as adults (8%) to say tobacco is safe.

Cannabis is now legal in some form in 23 states of the US. In the majority of these states, sales are restricted for medicinal use only, but in 2015 there will be four states where cannabis can be used recreationally. By contrast, cannabis is not recognised as having

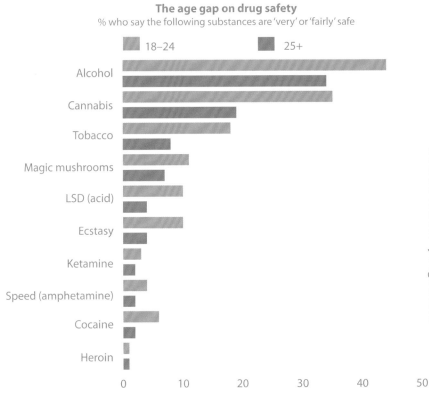

The age gap on drug safety
% who say the following substances are 'very' or 'fairly' safe

18–24   25+

Source: YouGov. yougov.com

any therapeutic value under the law in England and Wales, and possession carries a range of offences.

The differences between the legal systems have a marked effect on public opinion. In 2013, research by YouGov in America found people divided 45–48% on whether cannabis was safe or dangerous, respectively. In the UK, however, fewer than half as many (20%) say cannabis is safe.

30 January 2015

⇨ The above information is reprinted with kind permission from YouGov. Please visit www.yougov. co.uk for further information.

© Crown copyright 2018

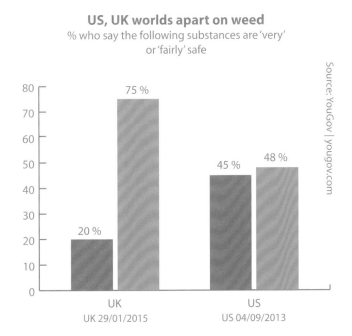

US, UK worlds apart on weed
% who say the following substances are 'very' or 'fairly' safe

Source: YouGov | yougov.com

UK — 20 %, 75 %
UK 29/01/2015

US — 45 %, 48 %
US 04/09/2013

Study finds link between teen cannabis use and other illicit drug taking in early adulthood

Researchers from the University of Bristol have found regular and occasional cannabis use as a teen is associated with a greater risk of other illicit drug taking in early adulthood. The study by Bristol's Population Health Science Institute, published online in the *Journal of Epidemiology & Community Health*, also found cannabis use was associated with harmful drinking and smoking.

Using data from the Avon Longitudinal Study of Parents and Children (ALSPAC), the researchers looked at levels of cannabis use during adolescence to determine whether these might predict other problematic substance misuse in early adulthood – by the age of 21.

The researchers looked at data about cannabis use among 5,315 teens between the ages of 13 and 18. At five time points approximately one year apart cannabis use was categorised as none; occasional (typically less than once a week); or frequent (typically once a week or more).

When the teens reached the age of 21, they were asked to say whether and how much they smoked and drank, and whether they had taken other illicit drugs during the previous three months. Some 462 reported recent illicit drug use: 176 (38 per cent) had used cocaine; 278 (60 per cent) had used 'speed' (amphetamines); 136 (30 per cent) had used inhalants; 72 (16 per cent) had used sedatives; 105 (23 per cent) had used hallucinogens; and 25 (6 per cent) had used opioids.

The study's lead author, Dr Michelle Taylor from the School of Social and Community Medicine said: "We tend to see clusters of different forms of substance misuse in adolescents and young people, and it has been argued that cannabis acts as a gateway to other drug use. However, historically the evidence has been inconsistent.

"I think the most important findings from this study are that one in five adolescents follow a pattern of occasional or regular cannabis use and that those individuals are more likely to be tobacco-dependent, have harmful levels of alcohol consumption or use other illicit drugs in early adulthood."

In all, complete data were available for 1,571 people. Male sex, mother's substance misuse and the child's smoking, drinking, and behavioural problems before the age of 13 were all strongly associated with cannabis use during adolescence. Other potentially influential factors were also considered: housing tenure; mum's education and number of children she had; her drinking and drug use; behavioural problems when the child was 11 and whether s/he had started smoking and/or drinking before the age of 13.

After taking account of other influential factors, those who used cannabis in their teens were at greater risk of problematic substance misuse by the age of 21 than those who didn't.

Teens who regularly used cannabis were 37 times more likely to be nicotine dependent and three times more likely to have a harmful drinking pattern than non-users by the time they were 21. And they were 26 times more likely to use other illicit drugs.

Both those who used cannabis occasionally early in adolescence and those who starting using it much later during the teenage years had a heightened risk of nicotine dependence, harmful drinking, and other illicit drug use. And the more cannabis they used the greater was the likelihood of nicotine dependence by the age of 21.

This study used observational methods and therefore presents evidence for correlation but does not determine clear cause and effect – whether the results observed are because cannabis use actually causes the use of other illicit drugs. Furthermore, it does not identify what the underlying mechanisms for this might be. Nevertheless, clear categories of use emerged.

Dr Taylor concludes: "We have added further evidence that suggests adolescent cannabis use does predict later problematic substance use in early adulthood. From our study, we cannot say why this might be, and it is important that future research focuses on this question, as this will enable us to identify groups of individuals that might be at risk and develop policy to advise people of the harms.

"Our study does not support or refute arguments for altering the legal status of cannabis use – especially since two of the outcomes are legal in the UK. This study and others do, however, lend support to public health strategies and interventions that aim to reduce cannabis exposure in young people."

8 June 2017

⇨ The above information is reprinted with kind permission from University of Bristol. Please visit www.bristol.ac.uk for further information.

Should the UK legalise cannabis?

***An Article from* The Conversation.**

THE CONVERSATION

Ian Hamilton, Lecturer in Mental Health, University of York and Mark Monaghan, Lecturer in Criminology and Social Policy, Loughborough University

A number of countries have decriminalised cannabis for personal use. None of them have descended into anarchy, so what's preventing the UK Government from following suit?

The Conservative government claims to be in favour of evidence-based policies – in rhetoric, at least – yet successive UK governments have signed up to the United Nations international drug convention, a convention based on prohibition and the war on drugs, neither of which have any evidence of working.

But does signing up to UN drug conventions matter when agreements can be sidestepped by individual states? Portugal's decision to decriminalise all psychoactive substances in 2001 being a case in point.

And Portugal is not alone. It is now 25 years since the Czech Republic effectively decriminalised the possession of small amounts of drugs for personal use. And in 1994, Switzerland introduced heroin-assisted treatment, a form of state-sanctioned heroin supply for certain users. But it is with cannabis that the most significant developments have occurred. In late 2013, Uruguay took the decision to legalise the recreational use of cannabis (as opposed to decriminalise where possession can lead to a fine, but not a criminal record). It was the first country to do so since the global drug prohibition framework was established by the United Nations in 1961.

Uruguay demonstrates that policy alternatives are possible without any international enforcement. Several US states have followed Uruguay, extending liberalisation to recreational as well as medical cannabis users. But the UK remains steadfast in its resolve, maintaining that current policy is working.

False logic

The UK is looking increasingly out of step with many other countries when it comes to its approach to drugs in general, and cannabis in particular. In the aftermath of changes in the US, polling suggests increasing numbers of UK citizens are also in favour of a change in the law.

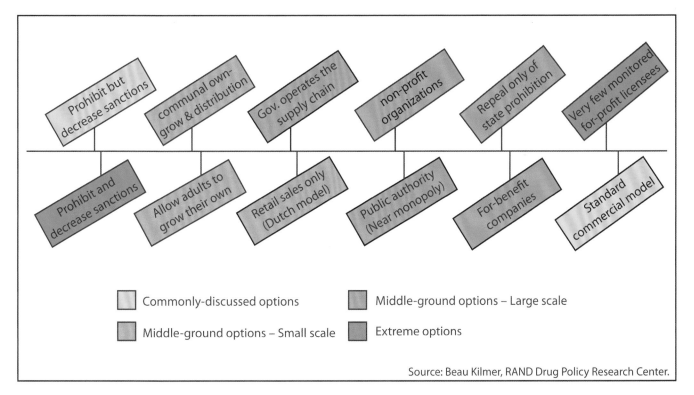

Source: Beau Kilmer, RAND Drug Policy Research Center.

The Home Office acknowledges that there is no "obvious relationship between the toughness of a country's enforcement against drug possession, and levels of drug use in that country". Convictions relating to cannabis use have reduced by 46% over the last five years. This could suggest that cannabis has been quietly and partially decriminalised. Yet the government maintains its outdated and dogmatic tough approach to drugs when making public statements about cannabis.

The Government claims that prohibition works because cannabis use has declined in the UK in recent years. This decline in use may account for some of the fall in cannabis conviction rates. But if we follow the government's false logic in relation to prohibition and simply wait for cannabis use to fall further, assuming it does (a very big assumption), then it would take a further five decades before their aim of eliminating cannabis use is achieved.

But such simplistic interpretation of the data is clearly wrong. Although cannabis use has fallen it ignores what is happening with certain sub-groups of cannabis users. For example, an increasing number of young people are accessing drug treatment services as a result of using potent strains of cannabis.

Individual and covert commercial growers have used advances in seed technology and access to hydroponic growing equipment to cultivate more potent varieties of cannabis. There is little doubt that stronger strains of cannabis elevate the risk of developing a range of health problems such as psychosis. Increasing potency is a compelling reason to change the current legal position, not one that endorses it.

What are the options?

Although the drugs debate is commonly framed as a debate of two extremes – legalise or criminalise – there are actually many options. For example, Beau Kilmer, co-director of the RAND Drug Policy Research Center suggests an incremental approach to regulation (see chart above).

This proposal could inform a new policy approach which has the potential to enhance health at a population level. Introducing state regulation would provide users with a cannabis product that has been tested for potency and supplied without the risk of harmful additives. It would also generate revenue, adding to our collective wealth. Evidence supporting such a change is accumulating across the world thanks to those jurisdictions that have moved beyond an ideological commitment to the drug war.

The Government's duty is to protect the people it serves. With cannabis it fails to meet this obligation in two ways. First, it outsources the production and supply of a widely used product to organised crime, meaning that there is no quality control or regulated standards of production. This leaves people who use cannabis conducting daily experiments with their health. Second, by publicly endorsing prohibition yet quietly allowing its agencies to do the opposite, it lacks credibility. It's difficult to work out who this policy serves other than a few elite criminals who control the production and supply of cannabis.

6 May 2016

⇨ The above information is reprinted with kind permission from *The Conversation*. Please visit www.theconversation.com for further information.

Legalise cannabis as treatment of last resort for MS, says charity

MS Society says there is sufficient evidence of drug's effectiveness to relax ban for patients with no other options.

Dennis Campbell, Health Policy Editor

Ten thousand people with multiple sclerosis in the UK should be allowed to use cannabis legally in order to relieve their "relentless and exhausting" symptons, experts in the disease have told ministers.

> **"The MS Society claims the one in ten sufferers of the condition whose pain and spasticity cannot be treated by medication available on the NHS should be able to take the drug without fear of prosecution"**

The evidence on cannabis' effectiveness, while not conclusive, is now strong enough that the Government should relax the ban on the drug for MS patients who have no other treatment options, the society says in a report.

Doctors who treat MS patients have backed the society's call, as have the Liberal Democrats and the Green Party. Legalisation would ease "the extremely difficult situation in which many people with MS find themselves", the charity said.

The society is calling for the first time for the 10,000 patients – one in ten of the 100,000 people in Britain with MS – to be able to access cannabis without fear of arrest. It has changed its position after reviewing the evidence, consulting its medical advisers and seeking the views of 3,994 people who have the condition.

"We think cannabis should be legalised for medicinal use for people with MS to relieve their pain and muscle spasms when other treatments haven't worked," said Genevieve Edwards, the MS Society's director of external affairs.

"The level of clinical evidence to support cannabis' use for medicinal purposes is not conclusive. But there is sufficient evidence for our medical advisers to say that on the balance of probability, cannabis could benefit many people with MS experiencing pain and muscle spasms."

The charity is also urging NHS bosses to make Sativex, a cannabis-based drug used by some people with MS, available on prescription across the UK so that patients who can afford it no longer have to acquire it privately, at a cost of about £2,000 a year. Wales is the only home nation to provide the mouth spray through the NHS.

Patients' inability to access Sativex on the NHS in England, Scotland and Northern Ireland "has resulted in many people with MS turning to illegal forms of cannabis as an alternative. It's simply not right that some people are being driven to break the law to relieve their pain and spasticity. It's also really risky when you're not sure about the quality or dosage of what you're buying," Edwards said.

Norman Lamb, the Lib Dem health spokesman, said: "This is the strongest proof yet that the existing law on cannabis is a huge injustice that makes criminals of people whose only crime is to be in acute pain. This draconian law is potentially opening anything up to 10,000 MS sufferers to prosecution, and underlines why the Liberal Democrats have braved a tabloid backlash to campaign for the legalisation of cannabis. It is about time the Government listened to the science."

One in five (22%) MS patients who took part in a survey by the society said they had used cannabis to help manage their symptoms, but only 7% were still doing so. A quarter (26%) of those who had stopped taking it said they had done so out of fear of prosecution. Another 26% of respondents had considered trying cannabis but had not done so for the same reason and also because they were concerned about the drug's safety.

Doctors are divided over cannabis' potential role in treating MS. Some are supportive while others are anxious about endorsing the use of a drug that can cause psychiatric problems. The Royal College of GPs said it was currently drawing up policy on the issue and could not comment. The Royal College of Physicians, which represents hospital doctors, said it had no policy on the issue.

Dr Willy Notcutt, a pain management specialist at the James Paget hospital in Norfolk, who has been treating MS patients for more than 20 years, said: "Every week I come across patients wishing to use cannabis to control their symptoms but who are unable to get proven drugs like Sativex from the NHS. Many patients seek illegal cannabis to get help. They can't be sure of its origin but are being forced to commit a criminal act in order to obtain relief."

Dr Waqar Rashid, a consultant neurologist at Brighton and Sussex University Hospitals NHS trust, said: "[Cannabis is] not a cure-all, and there are other treatments that should be tried first. But it makes sense for criminality not be a barrier to a treatment which could reduce the debilitating impact of symptoms and transform someone's quality of life."

Caroline Lucas, the Green Party co-leader and its sole MP, said: "The MS Society's new position is a big step forward, and recognises the fact that thousands of people with MS could benefit from the the use of medicinal cannabis. By rigidly sticking to criminalising cannabis, the government drives MS sufferers to illegally acquire the drugs, thus putting themselves at risk of prosecution simply for searching for pain relief."

The National Institute for Health and Clinical Excellence (NICE), which advises the Government, has told the NHS not to prescribe Sativex for spasticity because it is not cost-effective.

The Home Office said: "This government has no plans to legalise cannabis. Cannabis is controlled as a Class B drug under the Misuse of Drugs Act 1971 and, in its raw form, currently has no recognised medicinal benefits in the UK."

Case study: Steven Colborn, 55, from Seaham, County Durham

Imagine running a marathon while sharp pain darts up and down your legs. This is what multiple sclerosis feels like for me. When muscle spasticity kicks in my legs just twist and turn and bend back on themselves and it's excruciatingly painful.

But three years ago I was offered a treatment that could help. During a regular appointment, a specialist nurse said they had managed to get a month's supply of Sativex, a drug derived from cannabis, from the manufacturer.

The results were incredible. My muscle tension eased and I started to feel my legs moving better. I was able to get a good night's sleep. I could exercise without getting as tired as quickly. For the first time in a long time I felt that I was managing my condition.

My month's supply ran out and the drug wasn't available free on the NHS. I was offered a muscle relaxer called Baclofen which hadn't worked for me in the past.

> **"I have been forced to pay for this drug myself. I can't work any more so I rely on disability benefits. I have to save up a lot of money to be able to afford it – it costs £412 a month. Over the past four years I've only managed to buy about seven months' worth"**

I take Sativex but other people get similar relief from cannabis in its pure form. I don't like taking this myself because of the narcotic effect, which you don't get with Sativex. But for those it helps, it should be made legal.

I have had this illness for 36 years and every day I wake up and think "maybe there has been a breakthrough" I know there will never be a cure, but I am just looking for a way to make things easier. Now I have been presented with something that offers me hope and the NHS say they cannot afford it. My question is: can you afford people like me getting worse?

27 July 2017

⇨ The above information is reprinted with kind permission from *The Guardian*. Please visit www.theguardian.com for further information.

Cannabis legislation in Europe: an overview

An extract from an article by European Monitoring Centre for Drugs and Drug Addiction.

Brenden Hughes

What is cannabis and what are countries' obligations to control it?

Part one sets out to clarify the definition of cannabis. In this time of increasing debate about the legal status of cannabis, this is crucial to understanding some of the provocative declarations that "cannabis is legal" or "has been legalised" in a particular country. It examines what sort of cannabis is controlled, noting the different plant varieties, the parts of the plant, including the seeds, and the relevance of cannabis potency. It outlines how using parts of the cannabis plant for medical and industrial purposes is permitted under European or national legislation. It then focuses on the use of cannabis for recreational purposes. It outlines how the EU countries are bound to control cannabis following their obligations under United Nations drug control treaties. It describes the extent of those controls and the corresponding room for manoeuvre open to countries which choose to vary their legislation within those international obligations.

What sort of cannabis is controlled?

The cannabis plant is usually legally controlled when it is capable of producing a useable amount of the psychoactive substance delta-9-tetrahydrocannabinol (THC), but some countries control all strains, even those where the THC content is negligible. The plant has been grown for several hundred years for fibre, oil, medicines and drugs. Since 1961, international law has defined the cannabis plant as "any plant of the genus Cannabis", to cover the species *Cannabis indica* and *Cannabis sativa* and any variety discovered in the future. The roots and seeds have no THC, dried stem material will typically contain 0.3% or less, and the lower leaves less than

1%. However, in the female flowers, and the resin-producing trichomes (plant hairs) that grow among them, THC concentration can reach 20% or more. In the European recreational cannabis market, the flowers may be sold still coated with the resin ('herbal cannabis'), or the resin may be extracted and sold by itself ('cannabis resin'). By 2015, the mean potency of samples analysed around Europe had risen by 90% for resin and 80% for herb compared with 2006 values. In 2015, the estimated national mean potency of cannabis resin samples in the EU Member States ranged from 4% to 28% THC, while that of herb samples ranged from 3% to 22%.

The international treaties require that the entire plant is controlled under national drug laws, although in European countries there may be exceptions for plants which have a THC content not exceeding 0.2%, if grown for fibre. National control is not obligatory for cannabis seeds, although they are specified as subject to the drug control laws in Cyprus and Portugal. In other countries, supply of cannabis seeds for cultivation is often covered by a more general offence of 'facilitating drug production' or something similar.

Cannabis products: terminology

Cannabis products are used for medicinal and industrial purposes, as well as for intoxication. At least four US states and one EU Member State now have two separate distribution systems for intoxicating cannabis running in parallel, besides any industrial use of the non-psychoactive parts of the plant. Clarity is needed when discussing the laws involved.

Cannabis products that are used for medicinal purposes – whether the psychoactive THC or the non-psychoactive cannabidiol (CBD) –

are generally referred to as 'medical cannabis'. Cannabis products used in manufacturing are commonly referred to as 'industrial hemp'. Cannabis products used for nonmedical intoxication have been variously referred to as non-medical cannabis, retail cannabis and recreational cannabis. The term 'non-medical' cannabis does not make clear that it may not be for industrial purposes, while 'retail' refers to the form of distribution, rather than the motive for use such as 'medical' and 'industrial'. Therefore, this report uses the term 'recreational' for the psychoactive cannabis products intended for nonmedical intoxication.

Is medical cannabis legal?

International law does not prevent cannabis, or cannabis-based products, being used as a medicine to treat defined indications. According to the UN conventions, the drugs under international control should be limited to "medical and scientific purposes". Article 28 of the 1961 Convention describes a system of controls required if a country decides to permit the cultivation of cannabis that is not for industrial or horticultural purposes, while the 1971 Convention controls THC.

In European countries, authorised medicines may include THC in capsules, cannabis extract as a mouth spray, and dried cannabis flowers for vaporising or making 'tea'.

By contrast, no country authorises the smoking of cannabis for medical purposes. There are two main reasons for this. First, there are many strains of cannabis plants, and each variety has the capacity to produce a range of chemicals. The range and concentration of chemicals may also vary within one plant, for example depending on light levels during growth or maturity at, harvest. If these factors are not strictly controlled, it is very difficult for a prescriber and pharmacist to judge the content and thus the delivery of the particular chemicals needed for the patient. Second, inhaling smoke from burning plant material is not a healthy method of delivery of those chemicals to the bloodstream, as the patient will also inhale harmful tars and particles. When the required chemicals are not psychoactive, such as CBD, it is also very difficult for the user to measure the dose correctly.

A medicine based on cannabis extract has been approved by the European Medicines Agency, and at the time of writing four EU countries have specific legal processes governing the distribution and use of medical cannabis.

Cannabis extract is the main active substance in a medical product commercialised around Europe under the brand name 'Sativex', which contains equal quantities of THC and CBD. This medical product, which is sprayed under the tongue, has been approved by the European Medicines Agency only to treat symptoms of multiple sclerosis. It is currently authorised as a medicine in 18 European countries. In some of these countries, national health insurance systems will reimburse the cost under certain conditions, such as prior approval or prescription by specialists.

Since 2001, the Office of Medicinal Cannabis (OMC) has been the Netherlands government agency with a monopoly on supplying medical cannabis to pharmacies and general practitioners in accordance with the terms of the 1961 UN Convention. Producers are licensed by the Dutch Government and must sell all produce to the OMC, which then distributes it to pharmacies. The OMC offers varieties of medical cannabis, with different levels of THC (ranging from less than 1% to approximately 22%) and CBD (ranging from less than 1% to approximately 9%). These products cater for different patient needs at a cost of about EUR 45 for five grams. These may be prescribed for relief of symptoms arising from multiple sclerosis, HIV/AIDS, cancer, long-term neurogenic pain, and tics associated with Tourette's syndrome. Smoking is not recommended by

the manufacturer, and the preferred methods of use include inhalation from a vaporiser and infusion in tea. In theory any doctor may prescribe medical cannabis, but in practice only a limited number do so. As of March 2015, about 1,200 patients get their medical cannabis, with a prescription from their doctor, through the pharmacy. There is no reimbursement from the national healthcare system, but there may be some partial reimbursement by supplementary health insurance.

In the Czech Republic, the State Agency for Medical Cannabis was established as a special department of the State Institute of Drug Control. It set rules for e-prescription, pharmacies and so forth, but a special register only started operating in November 2014. Use of medical cannabis products is only possible in line with the Ministerial Notice of 2013, and the prescription should state the mode of use and THC level (up to 21%). Initially patient limits were 30 grams per month, but these were raised to 180 grams per month in October 2015. Currently only 16 specially qualified doctors, such as oncologists and psychologists, are authorised to prescribe cannabis, and only 26 pharmacies can dispense it. Patients must be aged over 18 years. The first domestic harvest was distributed to pharmacies in March 2016, with the final price to the patient being about EUR 3.70/gram (the average price of illicit cannabis in the Czech Republic was about EUR 7.40/gram in 2014).

In Italy, the Ministry of Health is the coordinating body for medical cannabis. From November 2015, the ministry can issue permits for cultivation, production, possession and use, and herbal cannabis may be prescribed with a nonrepeatable prescription; the use of cannabis is only for symptomatic treatment supporting standard treatments, where results cannot be achieved with traditional treatments. Eligible conditions are primarily spasticity, chronic pain, nausea from chemotherapy or HIV treatments, loss of appetite from cancer or AIDS, glaucoma and Gilles de la Tourette syndrome. Licensed farmers deliver the cannabis to the ministry, which

then allocates it for production. The pharmacist buys the active substance from the ministry with vouchers, and prepares magistral preparations accordingly. Doctors should prescribe the most appropriate genetic strain, dispensing amount and consumption method (vaporising or infusion in hot water only) for each patient.

In Croatia, new regulations entered into force in October 2015 that amended the Ordinance on classifying, prescribing and dispensing medicines, to allow the use of cannabis for medical purposes. Following the recommendation of certain neurology, infectious diseases or cancer specialists, medicines containing THC, dronabinol or nabilone can be prescribed, on nonrepeatable prescription, by physicians working in general and family practice, health protection of preschool children and women's healthcare. These medicines may be prescribed to relieve the symptoms of multiple sclerosis, cancer, epilepsy and AIDS. They may be in various forms such as teas, ointments and other extracts including galenical preparations; smoking or vaping herbal cannabis is not permitted. The prescription should state the amount of THC in a single dose, the number of individual doses, drug form, dosage and method of use; also, if applicable, the type of herbal drugs and herbal preparation which will make the main composition. Medicines containing THC can be prescribed in the quantity necessary for treatment up to 30 days. The total amount of prescribed THC in 30 days of treatment must not be greater than 7.5 grams.

As at January 2017, no domestic cannabis was being grown for this purpose, but medicines were being imported

Is industrial cannabis legal?

In the European Union, it is legal to cultivate and supply cannabis plants for hemp fibre if they have low levels of THC. The granting of payments under the Common Agricultural Policy is conditional upon the use of certified seeds of specified hemp varieties; only varieties with a THC content not exceeding 0.2% may be used

(EU Regulation 1307/2013). Payments are therefore granted only for areas sown with varieties of hemp offering certain guarantees with regard to their psychotropic content.

There is a procedure for the determination of hemp varieties and the verification of their tetrahydrocannabinol content. Imports of hemp are also subject to certain conditions to ensure the above-mentioned THC limit is respected (EU Regulation 1308/2013). According to the European Court of Justice, case C-207/08 (Babanov), the cultivation of hemp fulfilling the strict conditions above by farmers respecting all the other conditions established by the EU legislation cannot be prohibited in any Member State, if this prohibition conflicts with provisions of EU law or undermines the aims and objectives of these provisions.

New countries joining the European Union, in which it was illegal to grow any cannabis plant under the narcotic control law, have sometimes needed to change their law in order to permit this exception.

March 2017

⇨ The above extract is reprinted with kind permission from European Monitoring Centre for Drugs and Drug Addiction. Please visit www.emcdda.europa.eu for further information.

There is legal marijuana in the UK – so why is it hard to get hold of?

Seven years after the first cannabis-based pharmaceutical was made available in the UK – which helps Multiple Sclerosis sufferers – it still costs more than £375 for around 270 doses.

By Nick Thompson

It's around this time of year that weed smokers get their time in the hazy sun. Cases get put forward, people get high, and then the legalisation chorus dissipates into the background for another year. But cannabis has been available in medical form for seven years now in the UK, though you probably didn't know that, and that's emblematic of the issue.

GW Pharmaceutical's cannabis-derived prescription drug, Sativex, is popular with sufferers of multiple sclerosis, but it's expensive. In 2014, NICE (The National Institute for Health and Care Excellence) found it not sufficiently effective in treating muscle spasticity for its price. In 2017, it costs £375 + VAT per pack, roughly 270 doses.

That decision meant the drug, administered as a spray under the tongue, isn't available in England and Scotland on the NHS. In Wales, there's limited availability. MS sufferers here are only permitted the drug to control spasms, not to relive pain, once they've exhausted other medical options.

Why is the first cannabis-based pharmaceutical available in the UK so expensive? Why is it so hard to get? And what does this mean for UK cannabis prohibition?

Caths Evans is a tumefactive multiple sclerosis sufferer and founder of the Sativex Advisory Group (SAG). Evans told me how traditional medicines made her feel sick all the time, "like a zombie". Evans' condition is characterised by spasms and infrequent strokes, years apart, which have had an impact on her mobility, memory and ability to speak.

Sativex – which she's been prescribed since 2010, luckily predating NICEs decision – aided her symptoms dramatically. "[Before] I had this feeling down my left side like my body didn't belong to me… It's like a tingling sensation; anything cold would be painful on my skin. Rain was painful. Hot water was lukewarm to me. I would take things out of the oven without using gloves; it was quite dangerous for a time.

"But once I started using Sativex, it was amazing! The tingling had stopped almost, the spasms stopped completely. You weren't out of your head on it; it just made you feel normal."

Crucially for Evans, Sativex is still not half as readily available as it should be due to NICE's decision, and also because Sativex is only made available for MS sufferers in the UK, though it aids symptoms in other illnesses.

The price of the drug is unlikely to be an issue of pure unadulterated capitalism. Peter Reynolds, President of CLEAR (Cannabis Law Reform), told me the main reason the price is so high is because "the process GW had to go through in order to achieve market authorisation is so expensive".

But according to an MS Trust spokesperson, Sativex has always been scarce: "The local CCG tended to be reluctant to prescribe [pre-2014], though that might have been down to the reluctance of clinical commissioning groupss (CCGs) to prescribe things without any NICE guidance, and they came out against it, which obviously closed it down entirely." In medical trials, around half of the patients responded, typically in the first few weeks of treatment.

It comes as little surprise to anyone familiar with the pharmaceutical world that the cost of research, development and marketing ratchets up the cost of a drug. The issue is suspect however when you consider Sativex and its counterparts internationally are much more affordable. The difference in the UK, of course, is that possession of cannabis – a controlled, Class B drug – could see you charged under the 1971 Misuse of Drugs Act, although figures suggest an anaemic national police force pursues this course less than ever.

The price likely stems from the added regulatory hoops Sativex must pass through in Britain, as, according to Reynolds: "The exact replica of Sativex can be bought in medical marijuana dispensaries in the States for a tiny fraction of the price that GW Pharmaceutical charge for it," as they don't have to comply with the same regulatory procedures.

GW's Vice President of Investor Relations, Stephen Schultz, argues it's not the parent company's fault for the price discrepancy, nor is it avoidable, as another pharmaceutical company, Almirall, markets Sativex and "each country has its own pricing scheme".

Sativex is not currently available in the US, as it's not FDA-approved, though it is in phase 3 trialling.

In Reynolds' view, it's the procedures the Medicines and Healthcare products Regulatory Agency (MHRA) and other regulatory bodies use to test new drugs that are the issue. "The whole way Sativex is regulated is fundamentally dishonest. It's regulated on the basis that it consists of only two molecules: THC and CBD. Whilst Dr Geoffrey Guy, the Chairman of GW, is on the record himself saying – I have it confirmed in writing from him

– that it contains up to 400 molecules.

"The MHRA and conventional or pharmaceutical medicines regulators are simply not competent, capable of regulating a whole plant medicine.

"Every other jurisdiction in the world has set up special regulatory procedures around cannabis because it is completely different from pharmaceutical medicines."

In real, consequential ways, GW is trailblazing in a particularly fledgling and legally dodgy area in UK medicine. For Reynolds, it's all for the better: "I'm a great admirer of GW... I regard them as the people who, at great courage, and at great risk, have broken the UK cannabis prohibition. By playing the Government's game, by going through the established procedures."

There's an inherent tension in GW's founding motives, in that they recognise the therapeutic value in cannabis, but their niche exists only if cannabis remains prohibited. So it's surely not in their interests the British Government affects any law change, is it?

Schultz told me the situation in the US disproves that. "In the US, we don't see the relaxation of laws around the medical use of cannabis or recreational use of cannabis as really being any significant impact on our objectives.

"There are those who will use medical dispensary-based marijuana products [in the US], but we believe that most physicians and most patients desire a pharmaceutical medicine," said

Schultz. "Our objective is just to provide that option."

Speaking with Caths Evans and other MS sufferers, it's clear Sativex has been incredibly helpful in aiding symptoms such as muscle spasticity, whilst the drug doesn't bring a host of negative side effects like typical MS pharmaceuticals tend to.

But availability continues to be a fundamental stumbling block for patients in the UK, particularly in England, and that's a travesty for those that need it. The drug provides compelling evidence of the medicinal efficacy of cannabinoids, though in the UK at least it hasn't led to a wider medicinal cannabis framework, but it provides reason to hope.

With Sativex, it's as if cannabis has been repackaged and delivered in a bottle – arguably to circumvent the Home Office's blanket denial of cannabis's medicinal worth – but it still hasn't been enough. Seemingly thanks to powers beyond GWs control, Sativex has largely failed to leave its mark seven years on.

26 April 2017

⇨ The above information is reprinted with kind permission from *The Independent*. Please visit www.independent.co.uk for further information.

The tide effect

How the world is changing its mind on cannabis.

An Extract from an article by Boris Starling

The current policy around cannabis in Britain is a messy patchwork of legislation intermittently enforced. It places political posturing above public health and tabloid values above humane ones.

Cannabis is classified as a Class B drug under the Misuse of Drugs Act 1971. Drugs are classified "according to their accepted dangers and harmfulness in the light of current knowledge", with Class A regarded as the most harmful and Class C the least.

Governments of whichever political hue use these classes, in theory at least, to help set out their overall drugs policy. Cannabis has always been Class B except for a five-year period between 2004 and 2009 when it was downgraded to Class C before being reclassified as Class B. This was an episode itself emblematic of politics taking and discarding scientific evidence as it saw fit: in other words, of making the facts fit the theory rather than vice versa. Jacqui Smith, who was Home Secretary during the reclassification process, has since admitted as much. "Knowing what I know now, I would resist the temptation to resort to the law to tackle the harm from cannabis," she said. "Education, treatment and information, if we can get the message through, are perhaps a lot more effective."

Responsibility for developing and enforcing drugs strategy lies primarily with the Home Office, which in itself is a statement of purpose: that this is a matter of public order rather than public health.

The current government strategy is based around three main pillars:

⇨ reducing demand, particularly among vulnerable youths and/or those involved in the criminal justice system.

⇨ restricting supply by tackling the organised crime gangs which supply drugs through importing them from abroad or growing/manufacturing them on British soil.

⇨ building recovery in communities through public health facilities and an attempt to understand and tackle the wider social circumstances which propel people to use drugs in the first place.

Even the most cursory knowledge of British politics is enough to assess that all three of those pillars are built on very shaky ground.

Two million cannabis users alone shows that demand is widespread.

The rise in hydroponic factories in the UK, plus well-established criminal routes from the continent (used to smuggle not only drugs but also people), means that law enforcement is always fighting an uphill battle in restricting supply. And the social deprivation wrought on thousands of poorer communities across the land is not something which can be fixed with a few headline-grabbing initiatives.

Criticism of failure across all three of these areas is both wide and deep: it spans all kinds of stakeholders and goes back a long way. More than half the British public believe that current policies are ineffective – a figure which rises to three-quarters among MPs alone.

A Police Foundation report as far back as 2000 concluded that "such evidence as we have assembled about the current situation and the changes that have taken place in the last 30 years all point to the conclusion that the deterrent effect of the law has been very limited" – a point reinforced six years later by the conclusions of the Science and Technology Select Committee: "We have found no solid evidence to support the existence of a deterrent effect, despite the fact that it appears to underpin the Government's policy on classificatio.

When a policy of deterrence is no longer seen as providing that deterrence, those in charge of that policy's enforcement gradually decide that it's not worth their time and effort to pursue it. This is particularly when their own resources are scarce. Durham Constabulary, for example, have stopped pursuing and prosecuting cannabis users and small-scale growers. Ron Hogg, Police and Crime Commissioner there, said: "I believe that vulnerable people should be supported to change their lifestyles and break their habits rather than face criminal prosecution, at great expense to themselves and to society."

Nor is Durham alone in this approach: in Cambridgeshire, for example, charges are pursued in only 14% of incidents. But counties such as Hampshire, where 65% of those caught with cannabis end up with a charge or summons, continue to hold a line of serious enforcement seriously applied.

The problem with this system as it stands is twofold. First, it effectively makes the question of cannabis policy a lottery according to which county you happen to find yourself in. This is not the same as the case in the USA, where each state has its own legislature and where drug laws can vary widely from state to state. This is one national law selectively applied, which in itself makes a mockery of that very law.

Secondly, even the most laissez-faire constabulary when it comes to individual cannabis users continues to clamp down on the organised crime gangs which supply the drug. "The scant resources of the police and the courts are better used tackling the causes of the greatest harm – like the organised crime gangs that keep drugs on our streets and cause misery to thousands of people – rather than giving priority to arresting low-level users," said Hogg.

One can greatly sympathise with both Hogg's instincts not to ruin individuals' lives over something which harms only themselves and with his decision to prioritise finite resources on organised crime – the kind of real-world dilemma which all police commissioners face and which politicians and commentators alike are quick to dismiss.

But the endpoint of this approach is illogical to the point of absurdity.

Either a substance is illegal or it is not (or, more precisely, it may be legal in certain restricted circumstances such as for carefully assessed medicinal purposes, but that is a side point here). A situation where it is illegal to manufacture and supply something but not illegal to possess it is at best deeply flawed and at worst totally unworkable: the disconnect between the supply side and the demand side is too great. The demand continues to be met by organised crime: both law enforcement and health care remain in limbo.

This de facto decriminalisation is the worst of both worlds. The system as it stands, in general, works as follows. The first time you're caught with a small amount of cannabis, you're given an informal verbal warning. The second time, assuming it's within 12 months of the first, you're given a Penalty Notice for Disorder (PND) and £80 fine which must be paid within 21 days. Neither the warning nor the PND form part of a criminal record. Now the ante is upped. The third time is a caution following arrest, the fourth is a court charge. Both of these do count on your criminal record.

The problem is that even a warning, the most lenient and informal option, counts as a "recorded crime outcome" – a crime that has been detected, investigated and resolved. So cannabis crimes are a good, easy, predictable way for officers to make their statistics look good.

Every year, 10–15% of all indictable offences brought before the courts are for drug possession. According to the latest figures available, there are 1,363 offenders in prison for cannabis-related offences in England and Wales. Those 1,363 people are costing the taxpayer more than £50 million a year, are exposed to other criminals while in jail, are more likely to be recidivist offenders once out, and will find it harder to get a job in future because they have a criminal record.

The continued concentration of police efforts in poor areas helps perpetuate two forms of inequality. The first is that residents of these areas will continue to regard the police not as impartial upholders of law and order but as

agents of an establishment which regards them as at best a nuisance and at worst a threat.

The second is that the kids drawn into the criminal justice system this way – and the criminal justice system is like a lobster pot or the Chelmsford one-way system: it's very easy to get into and very hard to get out of – will continue to have far fewer opportunities for social mobility and life chances.

Would there still be cannabis criminals if the industry was legalised and regulated along the lines of tobacco and alcohol: that is, if it was well-regulated with licensed production and distribution? Yes, there would. But there are three main access points to such industries – production, distribution and possession – and only the middle one of these would afford any realistic opportunity for criminals. Possession would be legal, of course, and production (where most harm to the consumer's health in terms of impurities and toxins can occur) would be economically unviable for the vast majority of criminals.

Take alcohol and tobacco. Yes, there is smuggling in both cases, but in the vast majority of cases the products being smuggled have been legally produced at source and the smugglers are trying to avoid paying tax, which accounts for most of the price (averaging around 80%) of both alcohol and cigarettes in the UK. "Duty on cigarettes and spirits is consistently increased well above inflation, but the production cost of the goods is low. This makes them a prime target for smuggling," said Roy Maugham, a tax partner at UHY Hacker Young.

"A significant number of taxpayers are disinclined to pay the full duty on alcohol and, particularly, cigarettes – which has created a thriving black market. It's the inevitable result of heaping a heavy tax load onto any product."

In 2014–15 HMRC and the Border Force between them seized 5.3 million litres of beer, 189,669 litres of spirits and 1.49 million litres of wine, almost all of it legally-produced. There is no meaningful large-scale network of illegal alcohol production in the UK for the simple reason that legal, regulated, cheap alcohol is widely available.

Why go to the considerable expense and bother of making moonshine when you can just go down to the supermarket and pick up a brand of own-label vodka?

Cigarettes are a slightly different case. There are three main types of illicit cigarettes smuggled into the UK:

⇨ contraband (legally manufactured by major Western companies and paid at lower duty rates in their country of origin);

⇨ illicit whites (legally manufactured in developing economies, such as the UAE's Jebel Ali free trade zone, to product standards lower than in the West but still acceptable to most Western consumers);

⇨ and counterfeit (illegally made and passed off as genuine).

Of these three, the second category, illicit whites, accounts for the majority of HMRC seizures (more than 6 billion cigarettes between 2011 and 2015). "The illicit whites are now the dominant point of threat. They have none of the quality problems of counterfeit cigarettes," said Euan Stewart, deputy director of criminal investigations at British customs. As with alcohol, there is little mileage for most criminals to go to the bother of full-scale counterfeiting when there are so many easier ways to market.

The crucial aspect to this is that the very issue which causes the smuggling – the tax take – is within the Government's purview. It can intervene on price if need be, all the while mindful of the various stakeholders it must keep happy: the Treasury bean-counters, the shareholders of tobacco companies which themselves pay corporation tax and donate to political parties, the NHS which would prefer that fewer people smoked in the first place, and so on. The Government has no such luxury in a business like cannabis while it remains illegal. It can still enforce the law on the smugglers, but it can do next to nothing about the conditions which drive them to smuggle in the first place.

These black markets for otherwise legal products give us a good idea of what we could expect in a regulated cannabis market post-legalisation.

Clearly there would be similar issues with smuggling and customs evasion, but these would in turn represent a great leap forward from the current state of the cannabis market.

All the problems of this unregulated market come from a single source: the decision to treat cannabis purely as a criminal matter rather than principally a health one. Then Deputy Prime Minister Nick Clegg said in 2014 that "the first step is to recognise that drug use is primarily a health problem. Addicts need help, not locking up.

"It is nonsense to waste scarce resources on prison cells for cannabis users… (nobody should) go to prison when their only offence is possession of drugs for personal use. Instead, these people should receive non-custodial sentences and addicts should get the treatment they need to stop using drugs. These reforms will ensure that drug users get the help they need and that taxpayers don't foot the bill for a system that doesn't work."

Both the Royal Society for Public Health (RSPH) and the Faculty of Public Health (FPH) agree. In Their 2016 report, called *Taking A New Line on Drugs*, transferring drugs policy from the Home Office to the Department of Health is advocated;

"The time has come for a new approach, where we recognise that drug use is a health issue, not a criminal justice issue and that those who misuse drugs are in need of treatment and support, not criminals in need of punishment,' says RSPH chief executive Shirley Cramer. 'For too long, UK and global drugs strategies have pursued reductions in drug use as an end in itself, failing to recognise that harsh criminal sanctions have pushed vulnerable people in need of treatment to the margins of society, driving up harm to health and wellbeing."

Transferring principal responsibility from the Home Office to the Department of Health would also take away one of the arguments used by opponents of reform: that those who want cannabis legalised only do so because they erroneously believe it harmless. This is, of course, bunkum. It is precisely because cannabis can cause harm that it needs to have appropriate regulations and controls applied. Of course cannabis isn't completely safe. No drug is completely safe; no human activity, for that matter, is completely safe. But making it illegal doesn't make it safer. The Department of Health already provides information on the dangers caused not just by alcohol and tobacco but by sugar too. They are best placed to put cannabis in its context.

The time for a root-and-branch reform of UK cannabis policy is long overdue. Current policy emanates from the wrong government department and is aimed at the wrong kind of people. It is misconceived from start to finish.

⇨ The above extract is reprinted with kind permission from The Adam Smith Institute. Please visit www.adamsmith.org for further information.

Police chief slammed for turning 'blind eye' to cannabis

A police chief who said his force is not prioritising cannabis users who grow the drug for their own consumption has been roundly criticised by MPs, the press, campaigners and doctors.

This week Ron Hogg, Police and Crime Commissioner for Durham, said cases where the plants are grown for personal use are "unlikely" to be taken to court.

But he has come under fire for effectively decriminalising cannabis, which can damage mental health and lead to harder substance use.

Liberal elite view

Conservative MP Philip Davies, who is on the Justice Select Committee, said that Hogg is abusing his position, and

should try and get elected to Parliament if he wants to change the law.

And fellow Tory MP Andrew Percy said: "We've got to start debunking the liberal elite view that cannabis is some sort of benign drug.

"As a teacher, I saw very much how cannabis was a gateway to other, harder drugs."

Cannabis should be legalised for medicinal use, parliamentary group says

86% of patients experienced "great relief".

Kathryn Snowdon

Britain "lags behind" at least 11 other European countries and nearly half of US states as medicinal use of cannabis continues to be illegal.

Cannabis has been recognised as medicine for more than 4,000 years and was only made illegal in the UK in 1971, campaigners say.

But now a parliamentary group is calling for the law to allow patients to use the Class B substance.

A survey commissioned by the All-Party Parliamentary Group (APPG) for Drug Policy Reform found that 86% of patients who use cannabis experienced "great relief", with more than 90% reporting no or mild side-effects from cannabis treatment.

By contrast, respondents experienced "significant", "severe" and "very severe" side effects from prescribed medication.

The group is calling for the Government to introduce a system that allows people to access cannabis for medical reasons.

The proposal will put the UK in line with at least 11 other European countries, including Austria, Germany, the Czech Republic, Finland, Belgium, Italy, The Netherlands, Romania, Portugal and Switzerland.

A total of 24 US states also already allow access to the drug.

David Nutt, who was the Government's chief drugs advisor, said the pursuit of patients who used the drug to alleviate pain caused harm and wasted large amounts of money.

"Cannabis has been a medicine for more than 4,000 years, and in the UK was in the pharmacopoeia until 1971 when the USA forced us to remove it as part of the war on drugs.

"Now, over 200 million Americans have access to medicinal cannabis whereas we do not," Nutt told *The Guardian*.

Neurologist Professor Mike Barnes was commissioned by the group to review evidence collected.

Writing in *The Guardian*, Professor Barnes called on the Government to legalise the drug for medicinal purposes.

"My challenge to the Government is to have the political courage to accept the scientific rationale, accept the evidence and move to legalise access to medical cannabis under prescription here in the UK as a matter of urgency," Professor Barnes said.

The group recommended that the government:

⇨ Accepts that medicinal cannabis works and has a role to play in the treatment of a range of conditions.

⇨ Moves to introduce a system that allows lawful access to medicinal cannabis in the UK.

⇨ Decriminalises home growing of small quantities of cannabis for medicinal purposes.

The report estimates that 30,000 people a day in the UK use cannabis medicinally.

But campaign group End Our Pain puts the estimate much higher at one million.

The report said that a "sizeable population" of patients in the UK have found that medicinal cannabis works for them, offering relief from their symptoms.

The authors highlight that patients who require access to medicinal cannabis "have to suffer the added stress of breaking the law to obtain what for them is a medicine".

"The issue of medicinal cannabis should be treated as a matter of compassion and be viewed separately from the wider issue of drug policy reform," the report said.

13 September 2016

⇨ The above information is reprinted with kind permission from *The Huffington Post*. Please visit www.huffingtonpost.co.uk for further information.

Cannabis regulation and the UN Treaties

Strategies for reform.

As jurisdictions enact reforms creating legal access to cannabis for purposes other than exclusively "medical and scientific", tensions surrounding the existing UN drug treaties and evolving law and practice in Member States continue to grow. How might governments and the UN system address these growing tensions in ways that acknowledge the policy shifts underway and help to modernise the drug treaty regime itself, and thereby reinforce the UN pillars of human rights, development, peace and security, and the rule of law?

These treaty tensions have become the 'elephant in the room' in key high-level forums, including the 2016 United Nations General Assembly Special Session (UNGASS) on drugs – obviously present, but studiously ignored.

Different countries and international agencies have different reasons for seeking to avoid directly engaging the question of what to do about these tensions. But the kinds of treaty breaches that may have seemed merely hypothetical only a few years ago are already a reality today, and will not simply disappear. Under such conditions, it is not difficult to understand why many countries would prefer to avoid or delay confronting the treaty questions raised by cannabis regulation.

Indeed, such concerns go far in explaining the attraction of the legally fallacious – but politically potent – stance that the drug treaties as they stand are flexible enough to accommodate the regulation of adult-use cannabis. Different countries have different reasons for finding appeal in the notion of treaty flexibility. However, for governments for whom it would be politically convenient to maintain that cannabis regulation fits within the boundaries of the Conventions – especially the United States – "sufficient flexibility" could be read as covering cannabis regulation.

The fact remains, however, that the accelerating process of national reforms has already moved cannabis policies beyond the boundaries of what the Conventions can legally accommodate. To move the debate forward, this article aims to illuminate the available options for countries to ensure that their new domestic

cannabis laws and policies are aligned with their international obligations, thereby modernising the global drug control system in ways consistent with international law and the overarching purposes of the UN system. It is important to emphasise that treaty reform does not necessarily require negotiating a new global consensus.

TNI is also calling for a special advisory group to make recommendations on how to better deal with the contentious issues following the 2016 UNGASS, in preparation for the next UN high-level review in 2019.

18 April 2016

⇨ The above information is reprinted with kind permission from The Transnational Institute. Please visit www.tri.org for further information.

Ireland to legalise cannabis for specific medical conditions

Patients with multiple sclerosis, severe epilepsy, or undergoing chemotherapy could be given drug despite safety fears.

Henry McDonald, Ireland Correspondent

Ireland is set to legalise the use of cannabis for treating specific medical conditions, after a report commissioned by the Government said the drug could be given to some patients with certain illnesses.

The Irish health minister, Simon Harris, said he would support the use of medical cannabis "where patients have not responded to other treatments and there is some evidence that cannabis may be effective".

The report said cannabis could be given to patients with a range of illnesses including multiple sclerosis and severe epilepsy, and to offset the effects of chemotherapy.

"I believe this report marks a significant milestone in developing policy in this area," Harris said. "This is something I am eager to progress but I am also obligated to proceed on the basis of the best clinical advice."

Last November, Harris asked Ireland's Health Products Regulatory Authority (HPRA) to examine the latest evidence on cannabis for medical use and how schemes to facilitate this operate in other countries.

The study found "an absence of scientific data demonstrating the effectiveness of cannabis products" and warned of "insufficient information on [the drug's] safety during long-term use for the treatment of chronic medical conditions".

"The scientific evidence supporting the effectiveness of cannabis across a large range of medical conditions is in general poor, and often conflicting," it added.

However, it added that any decision on legalising use of cannabis was ultimately for society and the Government to make.

Harris said he wanted to set up "a compassionate access programme for cannabis-based treatments" and was now considering any changes in the law needed for its operation.

The new medical cannabis scheme will run for five years and will be constantly monitored by Irish health service experts.

The big policy shift came in the same week that the Fine Gael-led coalition in Dublin backed the idea of a "safe injection" room for heroin addicts in Ireland's capital.

The Temple Bar Company, which represents bars, clubs, restaurants and other businesses in the cultural-entertainment quarter on the south bank of the Liffey in Dublin, expressed opposition to locating any of the injection centres in or close to the tourist district.

The Temple Bar chief executive, Martin Harte, said businesses in the tourist centre collected 1,500 syringes from the streets around the area every year.

"We are bracing ourselves for an increase in the level of syringe disposals and related anti-social behaviour," he said.

"Addiction centres make no provision for what happens outside of opening hours… The Temple Bar Company is not opposed to tackling issues with drugs in Ireland, but we are opposed to proposals that exacerbate and fuel an injecting epidemic in Dublin city."

Last year, Aodhán Ó Ríordáin, the former Irish Labour party junior health minister, became the first politician to call publicly for a safe injection centre for the more than 20,000 registered heroin addicts in Dublin alone.

Ó Ríordáin also said he favoured making the possession of heroin, cocaine or other opiates for personal use no longer an arrestable offence.

Although he is no longer in government, after last year's election, Ó Ríordáin's suggestion of partial decriminalisation of drugs among users won the backing of rank-and-file police officers in Ireland, who said it would free up resources.

10 February 2017

⇨ The above information is reprinted with kind permission from *The Guardian*. Please visit www.theguardian.com for further information.

MPs call for legalisation of cannabis amid warning UK is falling behind in its drug policies

Cannabis is the most widely used illegal drug in the UK, with 6.7 per cent of adults aged 16 to 59 using it in the past year.

By Katie Forster

The UK should follow in California's footsteps and legalise cannabis, according to a new report into domestic drugs policy.

If cannabis were made legal and regulated by the Government, taxation from sales and savings on criminal justice costs could net the Treasury up to £1 billion, claimed the report, which has been backed by MPs from all the major political parties.

Cannabis is the most widely used illegal drug in the UK, with 6.7 per cent of adults aged between 16 to 59 using it in the past year, according to the Home Office.

"The Government strategy is based around three main pillars: reducing demand, restricting supply and building recovery. All three are failing," it said.

Instead, it proposes a regulated form of legalisation which it claims would ensure quality and purity and reduce crime.

Former deputy prime minister Nick Clegg and former health minister Norman Lamb joined Labour and Tory figures to argue that the UK should follow the lead of the United States, where recreational cannabis use is already legal in a number of states including Washington and Colorado.

Four further states, including California, voted to legalise marijuana in this month's elections, while Germany is preparing to legalise cannabis for medical purposes and Canada makes plans for all-out decriminalisation.

The Netherlands effectively decriminalised cannabis decades ago while Portugal legalised it in 2001.

Mr Clegg said UK ministers should start planning for the possibility of a legal market for the drug so as not to fall behind other nations.

"British politicians need to open their eyes to what is happening in the rest of the world," he said. "Cannabis prohibition is being swept away on a tide of popular opinion and replaced with responsible legal regulation.

"Now is the time for ministers to start writing the rules for this legal market, including age limits and health warnings, so that we can finally take back control from the criminal gangs."

Mr Clegg also wrote a letter to the *British Medical Journal* last week in which he claimed cannabis is "much safer" than many other medicines in use and said continuing to criminalise it was "absurd".

The new report referred to the "last major campaign to legalise cannabis in this country" over six months by *The Independent on Sunday* in 1997, which culminated in a protest in central London attended by tens of thousands.

However, it said the march organised by the newspaper was a "high-water mark of the campaign rather than a stepping stone in the stream of progress towards regulation".

The report argued that Britain's "dark ages" drugs policy has failed to stop drugs being manufactured and used, and to stop associated crime, corruption and killing.

It called for "root and branch" reform to legalise and regulate cannabis to ensure it meets acceptable standards, and to remove the market for criminal gangs.

A legal cannabis market could be worth £6.8 billion to the economy annually, potentially netting between £750 million and £1.05 billionn in tax revenues and reduced criminal justice costs, it said.

The report claimed the number of offenders in prison for cannabis-related offences in England and Wales would also probably drop from the current 1,363, who cost taxpayers £50 million a year.

Mr Lamb said: "Prohibition is harmful and counter-productive, helping neither to reduce drug use nor the risks to public health.

"While other countries and US states are increasingly coming to adopt a more enlightened approach to drug policy, we are stuck in the dark ages, filling the pockets of criminals and perpetuating the stigma which prevents so many drug users from seeking help."

Conservative former cabinet minister Peter Lilley, Labour MP Paul Flynn and co-leader of the Green Party Caroline Lucas also backed the report.

"The UK's 45 years of harsh prohibition has multiplied use and harm," said Mr Flynn.

"A legal market would destroy the drug's attraction as forbidden fruit and encourage users to ingest cannabis, of known strength and quality, in ways that will the avoid deadly dangers of smoking."

21 November 2016

⇨ The above information is reprinted with kind permission from *The Independent*. Please visit www.independent.co.uk for further information.

William discusses drug legalisation with former addicts

Prince William "could be a useful establishment voice for change".

By Stephen Hopkins

Drug campaigners have applauded the Duke of Cambridge for speaking to former addicts on the controversial topic of legalising drugs.

William asked three individuals, helped by drug addiction charity the Spitalfields Crypt Trust (SCT), about the "big dangers" of lifting the ban.

Prince William did not give his personal opinion but appeared to be on a fact-finding mission, telling the trio that after meeting them and touring the SCT in Shoreditch, east London it was a question "I had to ask".

He asked the recovering addicts: "Can I ask you a very massive question – it's a big one – there's obviously a lot of pressure growing in areas about legalising drugs and things like that. What are your individual opinions on that?

"I know it's a big question, but you seem like the key people to actually get a very good idea as to, you know, what are the big dangers there – what are the feelings?"

Prince William's interest in drug laws was applauded by Transform's Steve Rolles who said he could become a "useful establishment voice for change".

Heather Blackburn, 49, said she thought the legalisation of drugs was "a good idea" and that money was wasted on drug laws.

Jason Malham, 45, a recovering heroin addict originally from Melbourne, Australia, said: "Personally, I believe that they should not be made legal."

Prince William described his visit to the addiction charity as "a very useful little snapshot", telling those he spoke to: "You guys have seen it and it's affected your lives in ways I can only imagine, so it's very interesting to hear that from you.

"Talking to you and being here, it feels like a question I had to ask, I appreciate your honesty."

For more than 50 years SCT has provided services for addicts who are usually rough sleepers, something William is likely to have come across in his support for the homeless charities Centrepoint, in his role as patron, and The Passage.

William's brother Prince Harry was sent to a drugs rehabilitation clinic in 2002 after he admitted drinking alcohol when under age and smoking cannabis.

The Prince of Wales was believed to have sent his son to visit Featherstone Lodge Rehabilitation Centre in Peckham, south London, where he talked to heroine and cocaine addicts.

The Government said in its drug strategy published in July: "We have no intention of decriminalising drugs. Drugs are illegal because scientific and medical analysis has shown they are harmful to human health.

"Drug misuse is also associated with much wider societal harms including family breakdown, poverty, crime and anti-social behaviour.

"We are aware of decriminalisation approaches being taken overseas, but it is overly simplistic to say that decriminalisation works."

20 September 2017

⇨ The above information is reprinted with kind permission from The Huffington Post UK. Please visit www.huffingtonpost.co.uk for further information.

Marijuana as medicine

What is medical marijuana?

The term medical marijuana refers to using the whole, unprocessed marijuana plant or its basic extracts to treat symptoms of illness and other conditions. The US Food and Drug Administration (FDA) has not recognised or approved the marijuana plant as medicine.

However, scientific study of the chemicals in marijuana, called cannabinoids, has led to two FDA-approved medications that contain cannabinoid chemicals in pill form. Continued research may lead to more medications.

Because the marijuana plant contains chemicals that may help treat a range of illnesses and symptoms, many people argue that it should be legal for medical purposes. In fact, a growing number of states have legalised marijuana for medical use.

Why isn't the marijuana plant an FDA-approved medicine?

The FDA requires carefully conducted studies (clinical trials) in hundreds to thousands of human subjects to determine the benefits and risks of a possible medication. So far, researchers haven't conducted enough large-scale clinical trials that show that the benefits of the marijuana plant (as opposed to its cannabinoid ingredients) outweigh its risks in patients it's meant to treat.

Can medical marijuana legalization decrease prescription opioid problems?

Some preliminary studies have suggested that medical marijuana legalisation might be associated with decreased prescription opioid use and overdose deaths, but researchers don't have enough evidence yet to confirm this finding. For example, one NIDA-funded study suggested a link between medical marijuana legalisation and fewer overdose deaths from prescription opioids. But this study didn't show that medical marijuana legalisation caused the decrease in deaths or that pain patients changed their drug-taking behaviour. A more detailed NIDA-funded analysis showed that legally protected medical marijuana dispensaries, not just medical marijuana laws, were also associated with a decrease in the following:

⇨ opioid prescribing

⇨ self-reports of opioid misuse

⇨ treatment admissions for opioid addiction.

Additionally, data suggests that medical marijuana treatment may reduce the opioid dose prescribed for pain patients, and a recent study showed that availability of medical marijuana for Medicare patients reduced prescribing of medications, including opioids, for their pain. NIDA is funding additional studies to determine the link between medical marijuana use and the use or misuse of opioids for pain. Read more in the NIDA marijuana research report.

What are cannabinoids?

Cannabinoids are chemicals related to delta-9-tetrahydrocannabinol (THC), marijuana's main mind-altering ingredient that makes people 'high'. The marijuana plant contains more than 100 cannabinoids. Scientists as well as illegal manufacturers have produced many cannabinoids in the lab. Some of these cannabinoids are extremely powerful and have led to serious health effects when misused. Read more in our Synthetic Cannabinoids (K2/Spice) DrugFacts.

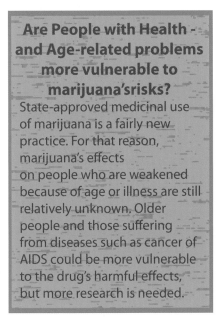

Are People with Health- and Age-related problems more vulnerable to marijuana'srisks?
State-approved medicinal use of marijuana is a fairly new practice. For that reason, marijuana's effects on people who are weakened because of age or illness are still relatively unknown. Older people and those suffering from diseases such as cancer of AIDS could be more vulnerable to the drug's harmful effects, but more research is needed.

CBD and childhood epilepsy

There is growing interest in the marijuana chemical cannabidiol (CBD) to treat certain conditions such as childhood epilepsy, a disorder that causes a child to have violent seizures. Therefore, scientists have been specially breeding marijuana plants and making CBD in oil form for treatment purposes. These drugs aren't popular for recreational use because they aren't intoxicating.

The body also produces its own cannabinoid chemicals. They play a role in regulating pleasure, memory, thinking, concentration, body movement, awareness of time, appetite, pain, and the senses (taste, touch, smell, hearing and sight).

How might cannabinoids be useful as medicine?

Currently, the two main cannabinoids from the marijuana plant that are of medical interest are THC and CBD.

THC can increase appetite and reduce nausea. THC may also decrease pain, inflammation (swelling and redness) and muscle control problems.

Unlike THC, CBD is a cannabinoid that doesn't make people 'high'. It may be useful in reducing pain and inflammation, controlling epileptic seizures, and possibly even treating mental illness and addictions.

Many researchers, including those funded by the National Institutes of Health (NIH), are continuing to explore the possible uses of THC, CBD and other cannabinoids for medical treatment.

For instance, recent animal studies have shown that marijuana extracts may help kill certain cancer cells and reduce the size of others. Evidence from one cell culture study with rodents suggests that purified extracts from whole-plant marijuana can slow the growth of cancer cells from one of the most serious types of brain tumours. Research in mice showed that treatment with purified extracts of THC and CBD, when used with radiation, increased the cancer-killing effects of the radiation.

Scientists are also conducting preclinical and clinical trials with marijuana and its extracts to treat symptoms of illness and other conditions, such as:

⇨ diseases that affect the immune system, including:

- · HIV/AIDS

- · multiple sclerosis (MS), which causes gradual loss of muscle control

⇨ inflammation

⇨ pain

⇨ seizures

⇨ substance use disorders

⇨ mental disorders.

Using medical marijuana during and after pregnancy

Some women report using marijuana to treat severe nausea they have during pregnancy. But there's no research that shows that this practice is safe, and doctors generally don't recommend it.

Pregnant women shouldn't use medical marijuana without first checking with their healthcare provider. Animal studies have shown that moderate amounts of THC given to pregnant or nursing women could have long-lasting effects on the child, including abnormal patterns of social interactions and learning issues. Read more in our *Substance Use in Women* research report.

What medications contain cannabinoids?

Two FDA-approved drugs, dronabinol and nabilone, contain THC. They treat nausea caused by chemotherapy and increase appetite in patients with extreme weight loss caused by AIDS. Continued research might lead to more medications.

The United Kingdom, Canada and several European countries have approved nabiximols (Sativex®), a mouth spray containing THC and CBD. It treats muscle control problems caused by MS, but it isn't FDA-approved.

Epidiolex, a CBD-based liquid drug to treat certain forms of childhood epilepsy, is being tested in clinical trials but isn't yet FDA-approved.

Points to remember

The term medical marijuana refers to treating symptoms of illness and other conditions with the whole, unprocessed marijuana plant or its basic extracts.

The FDA has not recognised or approved the marijuana plant as medicine.

However, scientific study of the chemicals in marijuana called cannabinoids has led to two FDA-approved medications in pill form, dronabinol and nabilone, used to treat nausea and boost appetite.

Cannabinoids are chemicals related to delta-9-tetrahydrocannabinol

(THC), marijuana's main mind-altering ingredient.

Currently, the two main cannabinoids from the marijuana plant that are of interest for medical treatment are THC and cannabidiol (CBD).

The body also produces its own cannabinoid chemicals.

Scientists are conducting preclinical and clinical trials with marijuana and its extracts to treat symptoms of illness and other conditions.

April 2017

⇨ The above information is reprinted with kind permission from National Institute on Drug Abuse. Please visit www.drugabuse.gov for further information.

Anxiety, chronic pain and nausea – the health conditions medical cannabis could help

Laws on medical marijuana are being relaxed around the world – but not in the UK.

By Lydia Smith

An increasing number of places around the world, including 25 US states, Canada, Israel and more than ten European countries, are relaxing laws on medical marijuana use – but Britain has yet to follow.

A group of MPs in the UK is calling for access to medical marijuana, in a report which called for the Government to view the issue as a matter of "compassion and human rights". The All-Party Parliamentary Group on Drug Policy Reform says there is "good evidence" cannabis can help alleviate the symptoms of several health conditions, including chronic pain and anxiety.

Professor Mike Barnes, a leading consultant neurologist who contributed to the report, explains how cannabis can help with certain health conditions.

"The human brain produces natural cannabis chemicals (the endocannabinoid system) and we are beginning to understand the importance of this system for human functions," he tells *IBTimes UK*.

"We now know that the endocannabinoid system has a role in pain modulation, movement control, brain adaptability (plasticity) and memory, as well as various endocrine, metabolic and immune functions. Our research confirmed that natural cannabis or synthetic cannabis products have an undeniable place in the management of chronic pain, spasticity (muscle spasm), nausea and vomiting during chemotherapy and the CBD component of cannabis helps anxiety."

Barnes adds there is also "pretty good but less strong" evidence for its use as an appetite stimulant, in epilepsy, for agitation in dementia and to assist with some aspects of Parkinson's disease.

One of the most common arguments against legalising medical marijuana is the association with mental health issues. Barnes disagrees that cannabis use – for medicinal purposes – is dangerous, saying it is "safe and well tolerated" and only around 10% of users report side effects.

He adds that concerns have been expressed about long-term problems and says it "probably" can trigger a schizophrenic episode in those who have had schizophrenia, or who have a family history of the condition.

Chronic pain

Studies have shown cannabinoids may provide relief to people living with long-term pain, including neuropathic pain. Some medicines, such as sativex – the first cannabis-based medicine to be licensed in the UK – are used to treat the symptoms of multiple sclerosis.

In 2010, a small, randomised, controlled trial of 23 people carried out by Canada's McGill University found those who received a low dose of inhaled marijuana – which was lower than the dosage necessary for a 'high' – reported a modest improvement in reported neuropathic pain.

Spasticity

Spasticity, one of the more common symptoms of multiple sclerosis, refers to feelings of stiffness, involuntary muscle spasms and pain or tightness in and around joints. In a 2012 study, participants with MS were given oral cannabis extract or a placebo drug for 12 weeks.

Muscle stiffness improved two-fold in the group taking the cannabis-based medication – and improvements were noted in body pain, sleep quality and spasms. There were adverse effects, however, including headaches, urinary tract infections and dizziness.

Nausea

There is good evidence to suggest that cannabinoids are beneficial in alleviating nausea and sickness as a result of chemotherapy.

Nabilone, approved by the US Food and Drug Administration in 1985, is a man-made drug developed from cannabis that acts as an antiemetic – a medication that acts against vomiting and nausea. It has shown some effectiveness in relieving fibromyalgia, a long-term condition that causes pain all over the body.

Anxiety

A study in 2014 highlighted the drug's potential in reducing anxiety. Researchers found cannabinoid receptors, through which marijuana exerts its effects, in a key emotional hub in the brain which is involved in regulating anxiety.

The researchers point out that although previous studies have shown the natural endocannabinoid system regulates anxiety and the response to stress, there is a catch.

"Chronic use of the drug down-regulates the receptors, paradoxically increasing anxiety," they write. "This can trigger "a vicious cycle" of increasing marijuana use that in some cases leads to addiction."

16 September 2016

⇨ The above information is reprinted with kind permission from *IB Times*. Please visit www.ibtimes.co.uk for further information.

© 2018 International Business Times

Cannabis oil prescribed on NHS in 'first case of its kind' in the UK

The medicine cannabis oil has been prescribed to a young boy with epilepsy on the NHS. Reports have called this the "first case of its kind" in the UK.

11-year-old Billy Caldwell, from Castlederg in Northern Ireland, has epilepsy and can have up to 100 seizures a day.

His mother Charlotte had previously got cannabis oil for Billy's treatment from the US. This medicine reportedly had stopped Billy's seizures. However, when they were unable to travel for a new supply, she took Billy to their GP. Reports say that in recognising this as a "unique" case, Dr Brendan O'Hare prescribed the medicine.

Cannabis oil is a medicine containing a part of the cannabis plant called cannabidiol (CBD). It does not contain the 'psychoactive' part of cannabis – the part that causes the feeling of being high. Last year, the UK's Medicines and Healthcare products Regulatory Agency (MHRA) classed CBD as a medicine in the UK. The agency has said that CBD products must be licensed as this means they "have to meet safety, quality and efficacy standards".

Dr O'Hare has said this was a decision to help a child facing a "crisis" and not a move to open the flood gates. However, campaigners for this type of treatment believe this is a big step forward.

27 April 2017

⇨ The above information is reprinted with kind permission from Epilepsy Action. Please visit www.epilepsy.org.uk for futher information.

© 2018 Epilepsy Action

Cannabis "safe to treat pain" but no proof it helps

"Smoking cannabis daily 'is safe when treating chronic pain – but only if you're an experienced user', study finds," says a Mail Online headline. It refers to a study done in Canada to see how safe medical cannabis is for treating chronic pain.

But the results of the study don't mean you should take cannabis if you have chronic pain. They don't show that cannabis helps to reduce pain, and the drug is also illegal in the UK.

In the study, more than 200 people with chronic (non-cancer) pain that had not got better with other treatments were given medical cannabis every day for one year. They were compared with a similar number of people who did not receive cannabis.

The study was designed to look at whether medical cannabis has any side effects – or adverse events – rather than its effect on pain. It found more non-serious adverse events in the cannabis group, but no difference between the two groups for more serious adverse events. It also found lung function test results for those who took cannabis changed very little over one year.

Cannabis use was associated with a small reduction in pain. But this wasn't the main outcome the study was looking at, and people weren't randomly allocated to the cannabis-taking and control groups.

This means it's not able to prove medical cannabis can reduce pain. Any small improvement would also have to be weighed against the increase in minor side effects shown by the study.

The findings are interesting and would benefit from further investigation with a large randomised controlled trial.

Chronic pain can be difficult to manage, and you may need to try different treatment options. Speak with your GP or health professional if you have chronic pain that isn't well controlled.

Where did the story come from?

The study was carried out by researchers from a number of Canadian institutions, including McGill University, the Jewish General Hospital and the University of British Columbia. Funding was provided by the Canadian Institutes of Health Research.

This study has not been reported widely. The body of the Mail Online article provides fair coverage, with a number of quotes from the researchers. However, the headline says "smoking cannabis", when only a quarter of the participants in the cannabis group chose to smoke it. Others used vaporisation or took it by mouth.

Also, it's not reliable to say the drug is "safe". People who took cannabis for pain experienced more adverse effects, albeit not serious ones. The study also can't tell us anything about the possible longer-term effects of medical cannabis on mental or physical health.

What kind of research was this?

This was a prospective cohort study investigating the safety issues of people with chronic pain taking medical cannabis for pain management, compared with a control group of people who did not take cannabis.

A randomised controlled trial would be a better way to investigate this as findings are more likely to be a result of the intervention, rather than other factors or the natural course of the illness, which may have differed between the two groups.

What did the research involve?

Researchers assessed 431 adults from seven clinical centres across Canada who had been experiencing chronic moderate-to-severe non-cancer pain for six months or more. Participants had either not responded to conventional treatments or were considered medically inappropriate.

Potential participants were excluded if they:

⇨ were pregnant or breastfeeding

⇨ had a history of psychosis

⇨ had ischaemic (coronary) heart disease or arrhythmia

⇨ had lung disease.

The intervention group included 215 people. 66% of this group were current cannabis users, 27% were ex-cannabis users and 7% had never used cannabis.

This group took quality-controlled medical cannabis (12.5% tetrahydrocannabinol). It was taken in whichever way the participant felt the most comfortable – about a quarter smoked it; others used vaporisation or took it by mouth. An upper limit recommendation of 5g was issued (the average taken was 2.5g daily).

32% of the control group (216) were ex-cannabis users, while 68% had never used cannabis.

Adverse events (serious and non-serious) were the main outcome looked at by the researchers. Other outcomes examined were effects on brain (cognitive) function, which was assessed using various memory and intelligence tests, lung function and pain, which was measured on a scale from one to ten.

Baseline assessments included addiction screening, neurocognitive testing, urine drug testing and, for the group taking cannabis, blood tests and lung function tests.

All participants were followed for one year, with the cannabis group receiving six clinical visits and three telephone interviews during that period. The control group had two clinical visits and five telephone interviews.

What were the basic results?

Baseline measurements showed the average pain intensity score at the start of the study was significantly higher in the cannabis group (6.6 out of ten) than the control group (6.1 out of ten). A higher number of control participants were using opioids (55% in cannabis group versus 66% in controls) and fewer were men (35% versus 51.2% of the cannabis group).

The rate of serious adverse events was not significantly different between the groups. A total of 13% of the cannabis group reported at least one serious adverse event, compared with 19% in the control group.

The most common serious adverse events in both groups related to the digestive system. For example, abdominal pain and intestinal obstruction each affected three people in the cannabis group. These serious adverse events were not considered related to cannabis use.

At least one non-serious adverse event was experienced by 88.4% in the cannabis group and 85.2% in the control group. However, the overall number of non-serious adverse events was significantly higher in the cannabis group (818) than the control group (581).

Non-serious adverse events that were very likely to have been related to cannabis use were:

⇨ drowsiness

⇨ amnesia

⇨ cough

⇨ nausea

⇨ dizziness

⇨ euphoric mood

⇨ excessive sweating (hyperhidrosis)

⇨ paranoia.

Analysis of adverse events against previous cannabis use showed people with a history of cannabis use generally had fewer events overall.

There was no difference between the groups for cognitive results after one year and, in the cannabis group, lung function results showed no significant differences one year on.

The cannabis group saw a significant reduction in average pain intensity by 0.92 points over one year. Both groups saw an improvement in quality of life.

How did the researchers interpret the results?

The researchers concluded that: "This study evaluated the safety of cannabis use by patients with chronic pain over one year. The study found that there was a higher rate of adverse events among cannabis users compared to controls, but not for serious adverse events at an average dose of 2.5g herbal cannabis per day."

They go on to say the study cannot address the safety of medical cannabis for people who have never used the drug. Further studies are also needed to assess the long-term effects of medical cannabis on lung and cognitive functions beyond one year.

Conclusion

This prospective cohort study assessed the safety of medical cannabis for the management of chronic pain. It found a higher number of non-serious adverse events in people who took medical cannabis daily for pain.

Outcomes for serious adverse events and cognitive function were roughly the same as for people who did not take cannabis. Lung function results in the cannabis group remained unchanged over the course of the year-long study.

Though the study was not set up to examine effects on pain itself, it did find an improvement in those who used cannabis. However, this result should be interpreted with considerable caution.

This was not a randomised controlled trial where people were randomly allocated to cannabis use (or not) to balance out any differences between the groups. There may have been existing differences between people

who did and did not use cannabis in terms of health and lifestyle factors, or differences in the type, quality and duration of pain.

This means this study is not able to prove medical cannabis can reduce pain. Also, it is difficult to know how meaningful a difference the pain improvement observed – less than one point change on a ten-point scale – would have made to individual people. Any small improvement would also have to be weighed against an increase in side effects.

Another limitation of this study is the large number of dropouts – 67 people taking cannabis and 34 controls – who left before the end of the study. Also, as the researchers acknowledge, though they found cannabis had no detrimental effect on brain or lung function, they did not examine this long term.

To summarise, the findings of this study are interesting and would benefit from further investigation in a large randomised controlled trial. However, for now the results do not suggest you should take cannabis if you have chronic pain. Nor does it confirm that cannabis is "safe". Cannabis is a Class B drug that is illegal to possess or distribute.

Chronic pain can be difficult to manage and different treatment options may need to be tried. Speak with your GP or the health professional looking after your care if you have poorly controlled chronic pain.

5 October 2015

⇨ The above information is reprinted with kind permission from NHS Choices. Please visit www.nhs.uk for further information.

Why is it still so hard for patients in need to get medicinal cannabis?

An article from **The Conversation.**

THE CONVERSATION

By Alan Wodak, Emeritus Consultant, St Vincent's Hospital, Darlinghurst and Laurence Mather, Emeritus Professor, Anaesthesia, University of Sydney

This week the Federal Government granted its first license for an Australian company to grow and harvest medical marijuana.

This follows Australia's amending of the Narcotic Drugs Act 1967 to legalise the production and use of cannabis for medicinal purposes. The amendment came in February 2016, a year after the death of campaigner Daniel Haslam.

Daniel suffered distressing side effects of chemotherapy, some of which were ameliorated by cannabis. While these changes sound promising for sufferers like Daniel, if he were alive today, he would still not be able to lawfully obtain medicinal cannabis.

Despite the media attention, extensive political and medical commentary on the subject, and the fact that more than two-thirds of Australians have supported medicinal cannabis for many years, a patient with a clear-cut and widely accepted case for being able to use lawful medicinal cannabis would still be unable to.

So far, only a few patients have been able to obtain lawful medicinal cannabis, and only after a long and difficult struggle.

Why is it taking so long?

There are a number of factors slowing down the availability of lawful medicinal cannabis in Australia.

With a multitude of natural chemical constituents, some of which are psychoactive – meaning mood, thinking and perception may be altered, perhaps pleasurably – cannabis is more complicated than most other pharmaceutical products. Cannabis can be used by way of a number of botanical products as well as partially purified or synthetic pharmaceutical preparations.

Much research is being invested in determining the components to treat particular medical conditions. For example, a widely studied cannabis plant extract has been used to treat pain resulting from nerve damage.

Since the mid-20th century, western medicine has preferred highly purified extracts of plants or synthetic products to provide greater certainty about effectiveness, side effects and dose.

Plant-based drugs containing mixtures of constituents such as omnopon, a painkiller derived from opium, and digoxin, a heart medication derived from the foxglove plant, were regulated and successfully used in western medicine from the 19th century until a generation ago when more purified preparations became readily available.

A political decision was made in 2016 that medicinal cannabis would be regulated through the Therapeutic Goods Administration (TGA), the section of the Australian Government Department of Health that oversees the regulation of drugs.

Although this may seem an intuitive decision, medicinal cannabis is very different from the usual drugs, such as antibiotics and diuretics, that the TGA has an excellent reputation for regulating. Because of its difference, some countries wisely created a separate Office of Medicinal Cannabis to regulate this drug.

By allocating medicinal cannabis to the TGA, the system is now skewed to an inappropriate, rigid and narrow approach that is also slow moving.

Consulting with those affected

Australia's response to HIV in the 1980s helped to prevent a national epidemic, saved many lives and saved billions of dollars. It was used as a model by other countries.

One of the fundamental principles was involving men who have sex with men, sex workers, and people who injected drugs in policy discussions. 30 years later, patients and consumers are not equal partners in the policy discussions about medicinal cannabis. They're merely occasional members of the audience.

Government officials, researchers and doctors joined by patients and consumers all working together will produce better and likely less expensive policy.

Most concerns are unwarranted

Some critics of medicinal cannabis have argued that its side effects, which can include drowsiness and slight euphoria, are unacceptable. But as with all medicines, what really matters is the extent to which the benefits outweigh the risks, especially in the context of a particular patient and their symptoms and condition.

Cannabis can have side effects, but these are generally fairly modest and certainly less serious than those of many medicines used for comparable treatments. Many commenting on the side effects of medicinal cannabis assume these will be much the same as the side effects of recreational cannabis sourced from the black market, and taken with the intention of experiencing the psychogenic effects.

But the side effects of medicinal cannabis used under medical supervision can be expected to be milder than those from recreational cannabis bought on the black market.

In a recent study of chronic pain treated with medicinal cannabis with 274 participants, nine had mild to moderate, and two had serious, side effects.

It's hard to avoid the conclusion that the perceived clash between medicinal cannabis and our decades-long commitment to drug prohibition is now the major impediment slowing the introduction of medicinal cannabis in Australia.

Government officials seem to fear that some lawful medicinal cannabis might be diverted to the vast black market for the drug. However, the Queensland cannabis market was estimated to have a similar value to the sugar or wheat market in that state. An economist estimated Australians spend twice as much on cannabis as wine.

It's time Australia took lawful medicinal cannabis for what it is: a useful drug to palliate distressing symptoms in some medical conditions when conventional medicines have failed.

The slower and more restrictive the system for medicinal cannabis, the more likely patients and their families will avail themselves of black market supplies. Given we can't be sure of the quality and safety of these products, and given the high street price tag, surely we can do better for patients in desperate need.

9 March 2017

⇨ The above information is reprinted with kind permission from *The Conversation*. Please visit www.theconversation.com for further information.

Cannabis oil stops life-threatening seizures in girl, 12, with rare form of epilepsy

Annalise Lujan is the latest child suffering from seizures to be treated with the cannabis derivative CBD.

Kashmira Gander

A 12-year-old girl with a rare form of epilepsy has stopped suffering from life-threatening seizures after doctors treated her with cannabis oil.

Annalise Lujan, from Tucson in the US state of Arizona, was participating in a gymnastics competition on 2 April when she was suddenly unable to walk, according to her mother Maryann Lujan.

The next morning, she was struck with seizures and rushed to intensive care where she was hooked onto a ventilator and put into a medical coma, KVOA reported.

Doctors at Phoenix Children's Hospital have since diagnosed the young girl with a form of epilsepy known as Febrile Infection-Related Epilepsy Syndrome (Fires). The disease affects only one in one million children.

The condition generally strikes children of school age, who suddenly suffer up to hundreds of seizures a day within a fortnight of contracting a mild febrile illness, like a cough or cold, according to the US charity RareDiseases.org.

Experts believe the little-understood condition is caused by inflammation in the body or a autoimmune disorder.

In a first for Phoenix Children's Hospital, medics sought permission from the US Food and Drug Administration and the Drug Enforcement Administration to treat Lujan with the marijuana derivative cannabidiol (CBD).

After 48 hours, Lujan's seizures stopped and she woke up.

CBD is an active ingredient in cannabis, but does not cause a person to become high. In a study by experts at New York University and Great Ormond Street Children's Hospital in London, cannabidiol was found to halve seizures in adults and children suffering with epilepsy.

"She was afraid. She cried. And, I whispered to her that she was very strong, she's beautiful, and she's strong, and she needed to keep breathing, and she did," Maryann told KVOA.

Lujan's family are currently raising money to continue her treatment using a GoFundMe page. They have so far received $16,700 of their $100,000 goal.

"It is absolutely heartbteaking and terrifying to see this helpless and innocent young girl stricken by such an insidious and devasting disease [sic]," wrote Lujan's second cousin Margaret Geittmann on the page.

"Any financial help received will be applied to her soaring hospital bills and rehabilitation," she added.

Lujan's treatment comes after the first NHS prescription for medical marijuana was given to Billy Caldwell, an 11-year-old with severe epilepsy.

3 June 2017

⇨ The above information is reprinted with kind permission from *The Independent*. Please visit www.independent.co.uk for further information.

Key facts

⇨ As with other addictive drugs such as cocaine and heroin, you can develop a tolerance to it. This means you have to have more and more to get the same effects. If you stop taking it, you can experience withdrawal symptoms, such as cravings, difficulty sleeping, mood swings, irritability and restlessness (page 1)

⇨ Smoking high potency 'skunk-like' cannabis can damage a crucial part of the brain responsible for communication between the two brain hemispheres (page 3)

⇨ The proportion of 11–15-year-olds in England who had used cannabis in the last year fell from 13.3% in 2003 to 7% in 2013. The proportion of 16–59-year-olds using cannabis in the last year has fallen from 10.6% in 2003–04 to 6.6% in 2013–14 (page 1)

⇨ High childhood academic at age 11 is associated with a reduced risk of cigarette smoking but an increased risk of drinking alcohol regularly and cannabis use (page 5)

⇨ Clever pupils were 50% more likely to use cannabis occasionally and nearly twice as likely to use it persistently than their less gifted peers (page 5)

⇨ Marijuana-infused foods – often called edibles – are becoming more and more popular in states such as Colorado, where recreational marijuana is sold (page 6)

• In the first quarter of 2014, the first year recreational sales were allowed in Colorado, edibles made up 30 per cent of legal sales. By the third quarter of 2016, that grew to 45 per cent (page 6)

⇨ In 2015, only 12.3 per cent of high school seniors believed that trying marijuana once or twice was harmful (down from 18.5 per cent in 2009). Less than one in three believed smoking marijuana regularly to be harmful, down from 52.4 per cent in 2009 (page 6)

⇨ Youngsters who regularly smoked marijuana are far shorter than their non-smoking peers. Boys who smoke cannabis before puberty could be stunting their growth by more than four inches (page 10)

⇨ 1% of young people say magic mushrooms are safe; greater than the 8% of adults who say tobacco is safe. And men seem more relaxed about drug safety, with 41% saying alcohol is safe compared to 29% of women, and 25% saying cannabis is safe compared to 17% of women (page 14)

⇨ Cannabis is now legal in some form in 23 states of the US. In the majority of these states, sales are restricted for medicinal use only, but in 2015 there will be four states where cannabis can be used recreationally. By contrast, cannabis is not recognised as having any therapeutic value under the law in England and Wales, and posession carries a range of offences (page 14)

⇨ One in five (22%) MS patients who took part in a survey said they had used cannabis to help manage their symptoms, but only 7% were still doing so. A quarter (26%) of those who had stopped taking it said they had done so out of fear of prosecution. Another 26% of respondents had considered trying cannabis but had not done so for the same reason and also because they were concerned about the drug's safety (page 19)

⇨ Britain "lags behind" at least 11 other European countries and nearly half of US states as medicinal use of cannabis continues to be illegal (page 27)

• Cannabis has been recognised as medicine for more than 4,000 years and was only made illegal in the UK in 1971 (page 27)

⇨ If cannabis were made legal and regulated by the Government, taxation from sales and savings on criminal justice costs could net the Treasury up to £1 billion (page 30)

⇨ A legal cannabis market could be worth £6.8 billion to the economy annually, potentially netting between £750 million and £1.05 billion in tax revenues and reduced criminal justice costs (page 30)

⇨ Studies have shown cannabinoids may provide relief to people living with long-term pain, including neuropathic pain. Some medicines, such as sativex – the first cannabis-based medicine to be licensed in the UK – are used to treat the symptoms of multiple sclerosis (page 34)

⇨ In 2010, a small, randomised, controlled trial of 23 people carried out by Canada's McGill University found those who received a low dose of inhaled marijuana – which was lower than the dosage necessary for a "high" – reported a modest improvement in reported neuropathic pain (page 34)

⇨ A study in 2014 highlighted the drug's potential in reducing anxiety. Researchers found cannabinoid receptors, through which marijuana exerts its effects, in a key emotional hub in the brain which is involved in regulating anxiety (page 35)

Cannabis

Cannabis is the most widely used illegal drug in Britain. Made from parts of the cannabis plant, it's a naturally occurring drug. It is a mild sedative (often causing a chilled-out feeling or actual sleepiness) and it's also a mild hallucinogen (meaning users may experience a state where they see objects and reality in a distorted way and may even hallucinate). The main active compound in cannabis is tetrahydrocannabinol (THC). Slang names include dope, ganja, grass, hash, marijuana, weed and pot.

Herbal cannabis [grass or weed]

This is made from the dried leaves and flowering parts of the female plant and looks like tightly packed dried herbs.

Medicinal cannabis

There is evidence that cannabis use alleviates the painful symptoms of some diseases, such as multiple sclerosis and arthritis. This is a controversial subject, as many believe those with debilitating illness should not be prosecuted if they are using cannabis for pain relief. However, others say that the law must apply to everyone or its impact is weakened.

Multiple sclerosis (MS)

A condition of the central nervous system in which the immune system attacks itself.

Reclassification

When an illegal substance is moved from one drugs class into another, after its harmfulness has been reassessed or new research has uncovered previously-unknown negative effects. For example, cannabis has been reclassified twice in the past decade, being moved from Class B to Class C in 2004 and back to Class B again in 2009.

Recreational

A drug that is taken occasionally and is often claimed to be non-addictive.

Resin

'Hash' is a blackish-brown lump made from the resin of the cannabis plant. In the past, this was the commonest form of cannabis in the UK, but this is no longer the case. Herbal cannabis (and especially powerful skunk strains) is now the most common form of cannabis used in the UK.

Risky behaviour

Behaviour that has the potential to get out of control or become dangerous.

THC

THC is an abbreviation of delta-9-tetrahydrocannabinol. This is the main psychoactive ingredient in cannabis and leads to the feeling of being 'stoned'. The higher the concentration of this chemical, the more potent the strain of cannabis. It is because of this ingredient that cannabis is one of the most easily detectable drugs when carrying out drugs tests, as THC can take weeks to clear from the body.

Assignments

Brainstorming

⇨ Brainstorm what you know about cannabis.

- What is cannabis?

- What effects can it have on people's health?

- What are the pros and cons of legalisation?

- What does the term 'cannabis psychosis' mean?

Research

⇨ Do some research into the usage of cannabis in the UK compared with other countries in the world. Draw a graph showing your findings.

⇨ Do some research into the medical uses of cannabis and the conditions it is used to treat. Write a one-page article about your findings. Share your findings with the rest of your class.

⇨ In pairs, research the different effects cannabis might have on women in comparison to men. Why does it affect the sexes differently? Produce an infogram showing your findings.

⇨ The article on page 6 discusses 'edible cannabis'. Do some research into the diffent types of food and drinks in which cannabis can be found. When you have gathered your results, write a short report about your findings and include a graph.

Design

⇨ Design a poster which argues for the legalisation of cannabis. It should show the reasons why legalisation might be a positive thing.

⇨ Create a leaflet for patients who are suffering from long-term pain. It should show the medical use of cannabis in pain management. It should inform them of the pros and cons of using this drug for pain relief.

⇨ Design an illustration from the article on page 10, 'boys who smoke cannabis are four inches shorter'.

⇨ Make an infogram from the graph which is shown on page 13.

⇨ Choose an article from the book and design a poster which highlights the key themes of the piece.

Oral

⇨ Hold a class discussion about the use of cannabis by teenagers. Discuss if you think this might lead to long-term drug use in later life and whether it would lead people into using 'hard drugs'.

⇨ Split the class into two groups and stage a discussion pretending you are members of parliament. One group is pro legalisation of cannabis and the other group is anti.

⇨ In small groups, prepare a PowerPoint presentation that explains the effect cannabis can have on the body and brain. You can use the article on page 1 to help you. Share your findings with the class.

⇨ As a class, look at the article on page 26 and have a discussion into the police not prioritising cannabis users who grow the drug for their own consumption. Give your views on this and discuss the long-term implications for this decision.

Reading/writing

⇨ Write a one-paragraph definition of cannabis.

⇨ Read the article on page 36 and write down your thoughts regarding the use of cannabis to treat pain. Consider the following:

- Does the drug actually work in the treatment of pain relief?

- Is the drug safe to use for treating pain?

- What side-effects might patients experience

⇨ The article on page 5 states that 'Clever teenagers are twice as likely to smoke cannabis due to their curious minds'. Write an article giving your thoughts on why this might be and if you agreee with this statement, giving the reasons why you do or do not.

⇨ Write an article for your school newspaper about the medical use of cannabis. You should list the ailments it might be used to treat and should give your views as to whether you feel it would be appropriate for the NHS to fund its use in this way.

⇨ Choose an article from the book and write a one-page summary.

⇨ Write a blog about Prince William's visit to talk to former drug addicts. You should give your views on the visit and whether you think such visits are a positive thing. What good do you think they can do? Should other well-known faces follow suit?

Acknowledgements

The publisher is grateful for permission to reproduce the material in this book. While every care has been taken to trace and acknowledge copyright, the publisher tenders its apology for any accidental infringement or where copyright has proved untraceable. The publisher would be pleased to come to a suitable arrangement in any such case with the rightful owner.

Images

All images courtesy of iStock except pages 1 and 6: Morguefile, pages 16 and 23: Pixabay: page 26 SXC Mateusz Atoszko.

Icons

Icon on page 5 was made from Istock.

Illustrations

Don Hatcher: pages 8 & 33. Simon Kneebone: pages 2 & 31. Angelo Madrid: pages 18 & 35.

Additional acknowledgements

With thanks to the Independence team: Shelley Baldry, Sandra Dennis, Jackie Staines and Jan Sunderland.

Tina Brand

Cambridge, January 2018